UNIVERSITY OF NORTH CAROLINA AT CHAPEL HILL
DEPARTMENT OF ROMANCE LANGUAGES

NORTH CAROLINA STUDIES
IN THE ROMANCE LANGUAGES AND LITERATURES

Founder: URBAN TIGNER HOLMES

Distributed by:

UNIVERSITY OF NORTH CAROLINA PRESS
CHAPEL HILL
North Carolina 27514
U.S.A.

NORTH CAROLINA STUDIES IN THE
ROMANCE LANGUAGES AND LITERATURES
Number 208

RABELAIS: HOMO LOGOS

RABELAIS: HOMO LOGOS

BY
ALICE FIOLA BERRY

CHAPEL HILL

NORTH CAROLINA STUDIES IN THE ROMANCE
LANGUAGES AND LITERATURES
U.N.C. DEPARTMENT OF ROMANCE LANGUAGES
1979

Library of Congress Cataloging in Publication Data

Berry, Alice Fiola.
　Rabelais, homo logos.

　　(North Carolina studies in the Romance languages and literatures; 208)
　　Bibliography: p.
　　1. Rabelais, François, 1490 (ca.)-1553?—Criticism and interpretation.
I. Title. II. Series.
PQ1694.B47　　　843'.3　　　78-24494
ISBN 0-8078-9208-4

I. S. B. N. 0-8078-9208-4

DEPÓSITO LEGAL: V. 552 - 1979　　　I. S. B. N. 84-499-2571-1
　ARTES GRÁFICAS SOLER, S. A. - JÁVEA, 28 - VALENCIA (8) - 1979

To the memory of my mother and my father.

ACKNOWLEDGEMENTS

My appetite for Rabelais was whetted in a seminar conducted by Professor Marcel Tetel one long-ago fall semester at Duke University. He has patiently and loyally seen my ideas grow from a seminar paper to a dissertation and, if that dissertation has now become a book, it is due in great part to Professor Tetel's steadfast interest and encouragement. My debt of gratitude to him is immeasurable.

I would also like to thank the Department of Romance Languages at Duke University for awarding me a National Defense Education Act (IV) Fellowship and for making the three years of my residency there so rewarding. I want to thank Professor Wallace Fowlie in particular, my great teacher, whose influence in these pages is pervasive.

Of my colleagues at Yale, I am particularly indebted to Professors Georges May, Charles Porter and Jean Boorsch who took the time to read with care parts of this book, to offer helpful suggestions and to give me great encouragement.

To my daughter, Vanessa and to my husband, Will, I owe, quite simply, everything.

A. B.

New Haven, Connecticut

TABLE OF CONTENTS

	Page
ACKNOWLEDGEMENTS	9
INTRODUCTION	15

CHAPTER

I.	THE RHETORIC OF SILENCE	33
II.	PARADOX AND THE CRITIQUE OF FICTION	53
III.	APOLLO VERSUS BACCHUS: THE DYNAMICS OF INSPIRATION	65
IV.	THE BIRTH OF THE "TIERS LIVRE"	80
V.	ORPHEUS AND ANTIPHYSIE: THE QUEST PERILOUS	99

CONCLUSION	119
SELECTED BIBLIOGRAPHY	122

He could galvanize the dead with his talk. It was a sort of devouring process: when he described a place he ate into it, like a goat attacking a carpet. If he described a person he ate him alive from head to toe. If it were an event, he would devour every detail, like an army of white ants descending upon a forest. He was everywhere at once, in his talk. He attacked from above and below, from the front, rear and flanks. If he couldn't dispose of a thing at once, for lack of a phrase or image; he would spike it temporarily and move on, coming back to it later and devouring it piecemeal. Or like a juggler he would toss it in the air, and just when you thought he had forgotten it, that it would fall and break, he would deftly put an arm behind his back and catch it in his palm without even turning his eye. It wasn't just talk he handed out, but *language* — food and beast language.

He always talked against a landscape, like the protagonist of a lost world.

—Henry Miller, *The Colossus of Maroussi*

Croyez que nous y eusmez passetemps beaucoup. Je vouloys quelques motz de gueule mettre en reserve dedans de l'huille, comme l'on garde la neige et la glace, et entre du feurre bien nect. Mais Pantagruel ne le voulut, disant estre follie faire reserve de ce dont jamais l'on n'a faulte et que tous jours on a en main, comme sont motz de gueule entre tous bons et joyeulx Pantagruelistes.
Je vous vendroys (dist Pantagruel) plus tost silence et plus cherement...

—*Quart Livre,* Chapter 56

INTRODUCTION

I

He was a veritable tower of babble. They had simply asked him to identify himself and he had answered most courteously, but in a language they did not understand. They asked again, and again the answer came in a tongue that was incomprehensible to them. Thirteen times they posed the same questions and thirteen times they could not understand the replies, until finally they asked him to speak French and he did. And thus it was that "... Pantagruel trouva Panurge, lequel il ayma toute sa vie" (P, 9).[1]

The meeting of Panurge and Pantagruel, like so many episodes in Rabelais, has as its center of gravity, language — the word for its own sake. It is the source of the comic, the focus of attention, almost the main character. Language is freed from the burden of signification and communication; words are piled up and played with for no reason at all, "for the hell of it," to use Spitzer's feli-

---

[1] References to the text of Rabelais are taken from: *Oeuvres complètes*, ed. by Pierre Jourda (2 vols.; Paris: Garnier, 1962). They will be in parentheses and will be included in the commentary. They will consist of chapter numbers in Arabic numerals and the names of the four books abbreviated as follows: *Pantagruel*, P; *Gargantua*, G; *Tiers Livre*, TL; *Quart Livre*, QL.

The critical edition of Abel Lefranc *et al.* (Paris: Champion, 1914-1965) was also consulted, as well as the following editions of the individual books: *Gargantua*, ed. by Ruth Calder, intro. and commentary by M. A. Screech (Geneva: Droz, 1970); *Pantagruel*, ed. by V. L. Saulnier (Paris: Droz, 1946); *Tiers Livre*, ed. by M. A. Screech (Geneva: Droz, 1964). References to these editions will be in footnotes.

citous expression.² They become, in the hands of the *maître ès langues,* a matter much like clay to be pulled and stretched and twisted at will into new and unknown forms signifying nothing. Their sounds are savoured, their senses are scrambled, and when the available stock of words runs out, Rabelais, like Panurge, unhesitatingly creates new ones — even whole new languages if it suits him. Why did Panurge use thirteen languages instead of answering directly and straightaway in French? Because it is the principle of his creativity that thirteen is better than one; that the multiple is preferable to the simple; that verbal *gaspillage* is infinitely more fun than verbal *économie*.³

And yet, the joy of verbal creation for its own sake is not unmitigated in the meeting of Panurge and Pantagruel as it is not in many of the other verbal phenomena in Rabelais's work. Spitzer has remarked about the speech of Janotus de Bragmardo (G, 18) that its very virtuosity constitutes a criticism of human speech: "... ce discours est démasqué dans sa nullité par le fait qu'il n'a aucun but, puisque les cloches ont été déjà rendues préalablement, et le discours même n'est que *flatus vocis* et cliquetis de mots... une caricature volontaire et parodique de tout langage humain, matière sonnante, sonorité fugitive."⁴ The same is true of the meeting of Panurge and Pantagruel. At the same time that there is manifest an enormous and voracious appetite for language, there exists a questioning of its legitimacy, an awareness of its limitations. Speech is praised in its fullness, but it is also unmasked in its nothingness by Panurge's verbal play.

First of all, his use of foreign tongues is not as gratuitous as it seems on the surface. His mystification has a pedagogical purpose. In Dutch, Danish, Greek and Latin, Panurge insists that "discourse is superfluous when the facts are evident." Particularly in the case of creatural needs (and this critique will be repeated in the epi-

---

² Leo Spitzer, "The Works of Rabelais," in *Literary Masterpieces of the Western World,* ed. by Francis Horn (Baltimore: Johns Hopkins, 1953), p. 145.

³ Robert Garapon, *La Fantaisie verbale et le comique dans le théâtre français du moyen age à la fin du XVIIᵉ siècle* (Paris: Colin, 1957), p. 10. See the Introduction, pp. 7-15, for an excellent definition and general analysis of the characteristics of verbal fantasy.

⁴ Leo Spitzer, "Le prétendu réalisme de Rabelais," *Modern Philology,* 37 (1939-1940), 145.

sode of Messer Gaster [QL, 57-62]),[5] language is not an aid to communication, but rather a frustration of it. Panurge's needs were immediately apparent to the group; his rags and haggard appearance expressed that he needed food and shelter. This message was clear; Pantagruel and his friends became confused only when Panurge began to speak. His incomprehensible answers parody their inappropriate and unnecessary questions, for neither questions nor answers were needed. Silence spoke louder than speech.

This critique of language derives from translating the ten real languages that Panurge uses. But the denser ambiguity springs from the three *baragouins,* fantastical languages, that are interspersed among the others. Their effect is to display the arbitrariness of linguistic convention, to show that all language, when looked at from the "outside," is *baragouin.* For the real languages are just as incomprehensible to the group as the fantastical ones. The only language which is meaningful to them is French, the language which Panurge calls "ma langue naturelle et maternelle." His reference to a natural language can only be ironic, following as it does a long sequence of languages whose effect is to show how "unnatural" language is when regarded from outside the culture which supplies it with meaning and coherence. For a German, a Scot, a Spaniard, a Dane, French would have to be included among the *baragouins.* Panurge is implying that there are no natural languages, that meaning is conferred arbitrarily by conventions of nations.

This implication also underlies another momentous encounter of Rabelais's *First Book,* the meeting of Pantagruel and "un Limosin qui contrefaisoit le langaige Françoys". Although this episode has traditionally been contrasted with the *Rencontre* because of the final punishment of the student, the two episodes are very similar. Chapter six also ends by identifying the concepts of "natural language" ("A ceste heure parle tu *naturellement*") and "maternal language" — the *écolier limousin* is exhorted to "parler selon le langage usité" of his native province. And, as in the meeting of Panurge and Pantagruel, this final exhortation seems ironic in view

---

[5] In his interpretation of the fact that Gaster has no ears and does not speak (QL, 63), Pantagruel repeats the theme of Panurge's Latin speech: "L'estomach affamé n'a point d'aureilles, il n'oyt goutte. Par signes, gestes et effectz serez satisfaicts..."

of the rest of the episode.[6] For the "langue naturelle et maternelle" of the student proves to be *baragouin* quite as much as his gallicized Latin, and both his *limousin* and his bad Latin are infinitely more fun and more appealing than either correct Latin or French would be. For his jargons incite laughter and even admiration; like Panurge, the *écolier* is a *forgeur de langues* "(qui) nous cherme comme enchanteur." But, also as in the *Rencontre*, the laughter and the charm are mitigated by the distrust of language that the *baragouins* provoke. They suggest that all language is fundamentally nonsense, that the sign is arbitrary and that meaning is relative to culture and dependant on convention. Pantagruel will make this case against natural language explicit and emphatic in *Book Three*: "C'est abus, dire que ayons languaige naturel. Les languaiges sont par institutions arbitraires et convenences des peuples; les voix (comme disent les dialecticiens) ne signifient naturellement, mais à plaisir" (TL, 19).

This assumption of the cultural relativity of meaning was one of the cornerstones of Renaissance philology,[7] and were it the only function of the *baragouins* to demonstrate this proposition, both Panurge and the *écolier limousin* could be seen as displaying the philologist at play with the many forms of human speech. However, his nonsense performs yet another function which undermines the "philological" one. The *baragouineurs* show not only that words

---

[6] Thus it may be argued that the *écolier limousin* sabotages the argument of the book which is commonly considered to be its source, the *Champ Fleury* which appeared in 1529. Rabelais's episode throws into doubt Geoffroy Tory's thesis that a correct, "natural" language is desirable, or even possible, and the "Ecumeurs de Latin, Plaisanteurs, Jargonneurs" that were attacked in the *Champ Fleury* are clearly given a privileged place in Rabelais's world. See, especially, Tory's "Aux Lecteurs...". The *Champ Fleury* has recently been reprinted: New York: Johnson reprint, 1970.

[7] Rabelais, a disciple of the great philologist Guillaume Budé, was engaged in philological studies of Hippocrates and Galen during the period immediately preceding the publication of the *Pantagruel*. Indeed, his translation of Hippocrates' *Aphorisms* was published in the same year as his first book, 1532.

For a study of philology as an epistemology as well as a methodology see: Donald R. Kelley, *Foundations of Modern Historical Scholarship: Language, Law and History in the French Renaissance* (New York: Columbia Univ. Press, 1970). The chapters on Lorenzo Valla, pp. 18-50; Guillaume Budé, pp. 53-85; and Etienne Pasquier, pp. 271-300, are of particular interest.

are arbitrary by conventions of nations, but also that they signify, or do not signify, at the will of the individual — of the *écolier limousin*, of Panurge, indeed of the writer François Rabelais. The encounter of Panurge and Pantagruel in particular shows how great is his power to establish conventions of his own. He can create new languages or subtract meaning from linguistic conventions that now exist. He may even, if he chooses, take meaning away from Panurge's "natural" language, and French is made into *baragouin* in the episode which follows the meeting of Panurge and Pantagruel, the trial of Baisecul and Humesvesne (P, 10-13). And it is by drawing attention to his own personal power to do as he likes with words that he casts serious doubt on their capacity to express the conventional which the philologist would designate as their domain. Rabelais's constant demonstration of his power to manipulate language for his own pleasure and to his own ends casts doubt on its capacity to truly signify anything at all.

Verbal creation is always involved to some extent in the ambiguity which surrounds it in the two *Rencontres*, for it displays the fundamental "unseriousness" of language, its "playfulness" and thus is doomed to both praise words and point out their limitations. This ambiguity is not always crucial — language is often sufficient unto itself in these books as pure entertainment. Yet, at the same time, there is a persistent effort on the part of Rabelais's characters to use language seriously, and when this is so, the ambiguity of attitude toward language becomes very dense indeed. We began with the meeting of Panurge and Pantagruel not only because the problem of speech is displayed there, but also because the circumstances under which that problem is most crucial are indicated. Panurge and Pantagruel meet on the road. The beginning of their friendship marks the beginning of a long voyage in quest of an Answer, in quest of truth. And it is above all when the quest for truth [8] is the

---

[8] This is the quest which dominates the *Tiers Livre* and the *Quart Livre*. It is to be distinguished from the parody of the heroic quest which is the frame of the first two books — the birth of the hero, his setting forth and his exploits. The proper medieval prototype for *Books Three* and *Four* would rather be the Grail Romances, with the Grail become the *Dive Bouteille*, the symbol of the thirst for truth. See: Nemours H. Clement, *The Influence of the Arthurian Romances on the Five Books of Rabelais* (Berkeley: Univ. of California Press, 1926). Paul R. Lonigan, "Rabelais' Pantagruélion", *Studi Francesi*, 12 (1968), 73, n. 6, also suggests this interpretation.

dominant theme in Rabelais's four books[9] that the legitimacy of language is most seriously questioned and the limits of its power are drawn.

II

The quest for truth is introduced into Rabelais's world just a few pages after the *Rencontre* when the Englishman Thaumaste comes to the giant in quest of "la verité seule" (P, 18-20). He wants to debate with Pantagruel, but he insists that they avoid language and communicate in silence using gesture and mime: "... car les matieres sont tant ardues que les parolles humaines ne seroyent suffisantes à les expliquer à mon plaisir." (P, 18). Pantagruel accepts this condition and he is, in general, quite respectful of Thaumaste and sympathetic to his concerns. In fact, Pantagruel takes the Englishman so seriously that the episode cannot be comic as long as he is the protagonist. Panurge must step in to conduct the *débat par signes,* and here Thaumaste and his quest are resolutely and emphatically ridiculed. This episode is thereby divided into two parts where two contradictory attitudes toward the quest and toward language are displayed.

The quest for truth as such is largely absent from the *Gargantua.* However, its famous Prologue and the two enigmatic poems which encircle the narrative, *Les Fanfreluches antidotées* (G, 2) and *L'Enigme en prophetie* (G, 58) all center on the problem of hidden meanings and of interpretation and these matters are always related to the quest for truth. All three episodes play on the paradoxical relationship between appearance and reality in such a way that the dilemma is given linguistic and literary as well as philosophic dimensions. They all focus on literature — on the meaning of the book and the poems, and on the way that language is used there. The first argument of the Prologue and the first interpretation of the *Enigme* assure us, in the manner of Thaumaste, that the matters dealt with are too important, "tant ardues," for straightforward speech. Hence, we must interpret the text symbolically and heed

---

[9] The *Fifth Book* will not be considered in this study because of the problems surrounding its authenticity. See our "Conclusion," pp. 119-121.

not the words but the silence behind them. Then, abruptly, we are assured of the contrary proposition, one which is similar to Panurge's "message" in the *débat par signes* — that the truth of life and of literature lies in what is tangible and concrete, in the word-as-it-is. And human words, Frère Jean insists, are play; moreover, the game is an end in itself. *Et tout finit en queue de poisson.*

In the *Tiers Livre*, the problems of truth and of language are no longer episodic concerns. They are at the heart of the matter and all the book is infused with ambiguity. The *Tiers Livre* combines the *procédé Thaumaste* with the format of the *Enigme en prophetie* in such a way that interpretation, that linguistic and literary dilemma, becomes the very condition of the philosophic quest. It is no mistake that the first oracle that Panurge and Pantagruel consult together is a book, the Homeric and Virgilian lots (TL, 10-12), for the world of the *Tiers Livre* is constituted as a text, one written in symbols and ciphers.[10] Most of the consultants avoid using language in a straightforward way; they prefer enigmas or symbolic gestures to speech. The quester after truth must therefore function as a literary critic or as a poet according to Baudelaire, he must pass through a "forêt de symboles" and gloss the Book of the World. This proves to be no easy matter, for when the group reverts to discursive language to interpret the symbols, they find that all of the oracles lend themselves quite neatly to two or more verbal interpretations. Those consultants who use language "reasonably" contradict themselves and each other.[11] It is to escape from this vicious verbal circle that Panurge sets them out to sail toward the *Dive Bouteille* who will pronounce the one irrefutable, unambiguous Word.

It is quite near the end of that sea voyage that the group sails into the Frozen Sea and encounters a deeply mysterious adventure, *Les Parolles gelées* (QL, 55-56). And it is here that the problem of

---

[10] For a discussion of the Book as Symbol, see E. R. Curtius, *European Literature and the Latin Middle Ages*, tr. by Willard Trask (New York: Pantheon Books, 1953), pp. 302-347. According to him, the book of the world as *illegible* is a variant of this image, one which derives from the Italian and Spanish Renaissance (pp. 345-346). The more widespread view was that the book of the world could be easily read, the idea being to "(shake) off the dust of yellow parchments and (begin) instead to read in the book of nature or the world." (p. 319.)

[11] See: Walter Kaiser, *Praisers of Folly: Erasmus, Rabelais, Shakespeare* (Cambridge, Mass.: Harvard Univ. Press, 1963), pp. 151-162.

language receives its most intriguing, its most suggestive treatment. This episode is a play on crucial comparisons and contrasts: the frozen words versus the thawed words; *les parolles* versus "le mot de la dive Bouteille." And each of the opposites is itself a focus of ambivalence. Pantagruel is most fascinated by the words in their frozen state, words only dimly perceived, potential words (55). When the *parolles gelées* thaw and burst, he is not only disinterested in them, he is openly disdainful. He tells Panurge that silence is dearer than this *baragouin* (56).

Panurge, to the contrary, is terrified of the frozen words, but he and another character called Alcofribas are ecstatic over *les parolles dégelées*. These are marvelous playthings that they would play with and pickle and keep forever if they could. Yet it is also Panurge who brings the entire episode to bear on the distinction between *parolles* and *le mot*. After a bitter and confusing argument with Frère Jean, Panurge rejects the thawed words that he had so cherished and expresses his nostalgia for the Word that transcends them: "Pleust à Dieu que icy, sans plus avant proceder, j'eusse le mot de la dive Bouteille" (56).

When Jean Guiton studied this episode more than thirty years ago,[12] he was fascinated by the paradox of the creative writer who is ambivalent toward language, the very stuff of his trade. He was also intrigued by the fact that this paradox is developed in an atmosphere that is Platonic — Guiton went so far as to suggest that this episode might be read as a "fable platonicienne."[13] There is good justification for this, for the myth of the Frozen Words is attributed to Plato,[14] and when Pantagruel first begins to speculate on their nature and place of origin, he begins with this broad philosophic statement:

> J'ay leu qu'un Philosophe, nommé Petron, estoyt en ceste opinion que feussent plusieurs mondes soy touchans les uns

---

[12] Jean Guiton, "Le Mythe des paroles gelées," *Romanic Review*, 31 (1940), 3-15.

[13] *Ibid.*, 9, note 23.

[14] "D'adventaige Antiphanes disoit la doctrine de Platon es parolles estre semblable, lesquelles en quelque contrée, on temps du fort hyver, lors que sont proferées, gelent et glassent à la froydeur de l'air, et ne sont ouyes. Semblablement ce que Platon enseignoyt es jeunes enfans, à peine estre d'iceulx entendu lors que estoient vieulx devenuz" (QL, 55). Rabelais read this in Plutarch's *De profectibus in virtute*, 7.

les aultres en figure triangulaire aequilaterale, en la pate et centre des quelz disoit estre le manoir de Verité, et là habiter les Parolles, les Idées, les Exemplaires et protraictz de toutes choses passées et futures: autour d'icelles estre le Siecle. Et en certaines années, par longs intervalles, part d'icelles tomber sus les humains comme catarrhes..., part là rester reservée pour l'advenir, jusques à la consommation du Siecle.[15]

The quest for the *dive Bouteille* is here placed by Pantagruel in a clearly Platonic context. He seems to conceive of it as a journey to the world of Ideas, for Petron's "manoir de Verité" recalls Plato's Plain of Truth (*Phaedrus* 248b) and the "intelligible place" (*Republic* 509d, 517b) where the Forms, the Exemplars, reside. But Pantagruel seeks *Parolles* in addition to the Forms, and this quality is not mentioned in Plato. It is of great significance that Pantagruel identifies Words with Ideas and makes them equal as the objects of knowledge. These are the Words he is seeking on this voyage, Words falling from the world of Ideas; Words which when thawed will bring truth.

Moreover, the *Parolles* which are the objects of the quest stand in contrast to those described in Plato's *doctrine es parolles* (see above n. 14). This anecdote attributes to Plato an ambivalent, if not a negative attitude toward language. Words are very problematic in the myth of the *Paroles gelées*, which expresses metaphorically both the difficulty of communicating with words and of understanding through words. Whether or not this myth bears any authentic relationship to Plato's philosophy of language will be studied subsequently. But what is important here is that Pantagruel places in a Platonic context not only the quest for the Word, but also the sense of the limits of human words which generates that quest. This episode does indeed read like a "fable platonicienne."

And what is true of *Les Parolles gelées* is true of all the episodes that have been cited. The quest for truth and the problem of language are always worked out in an atmosphere of Platonism. There are more than thirty references to either Plato or Socrates in Rabelais's work and innumerable references to the Neo-platonists: to

---

[15] This, too, is based on Plutarch, *De Oraculorum Defectu*, 22. Petron is named in 23.

Plotinus, Proclus, Iamblichus; to Dionysius the Aeropagite; to Pico and to the key names associated with Platonism in the Renaissance: Pythagoras, Orpheus, Hermes. And these names tend to cluster in the episodes that have been mentioned. The Prologue to *Gargantua* of course, centers on the figure of Socrates as he is described by Alcibiades in *The Banquet.* Thaumaste refers to Plato twice. He also refers to Pico della Mirandola and to Pythagoras, and Pantagruel reads books to prepare for the debate whose general subject is "Sur les choses indicibles," written by such notable Neo-platonists as Plotinus and Proclus (P, 18). In the *Tiers Livre,* the most Platonically-oriented of all the books, dedicated to Marguerite de Navarre, and concerned in part with the nature of women which was one of the major concerns of Neo-platonism in the sixteenth century, there are twelve direct mentions of Plato or Socrates. In fact, there is scarcely a consultation which does not allude to Platonic thought in some way. In the *Quart Livre,* in addition to the *Parolles gelées,* the episode on the Isle des Macraeons (25-28) may be mentioned, as well as the discussion of the names Riflandouille and Tailleboudin where Plato's *Cratylus* is discussed (37). It is as Abel LeFranc suggested in 1901 and as others have reiterated since him, these books are very deeply penetrated with platonic and Neo-platonic thought.[16] That tradition must now be examined in order to under-

---

[16] LeFranc set forth his views in "Le Platon de Rabelais," *Bulletin du Bibliophile et du Bibliothécaire* (1901), 105-114, 169-181. See also: "Le Platonisme et la littérature en France," in *Grands écrivains français de la Renaissance* (Paris: Champion, 1914), pp. 63-137.

As the reader is doubtless aware, LeFranc's colleague, Jean Plattard, contested his judgment and set in motion the long "querelle du platonisme" between them. Plattard examined every reference to prove that they were all second-hand and he concluded in his turn that there was no evidence whatsoever to prove that Rabelais had ever studied Plato with particular fervor. See: *L'Invention et la composition dans l'oeuvre de Rabelais* (Paris: Champion, 1909), pp. 221-225.

Plattard's opinion prevailed over that of LeFranc for some fifty years, albeit in a more moderate form. Alban Krailsheimer, for example, agrees with Plattard that Rabelais's Platonism depends greatly on secondary sources (Cicero and Plutarch in particular), but he also insists that this does not necessarily preclude a direct knowledge of Plato's doctrine. Indeed, Krailsheimer finds that Rabelais did have a good understanding of the theories of Reminiscence and the immortality of the soul, as well as of the theory of Idea. See: *Rabelais and the Franciscans* (Oxford: Clarendon Press, 1963), pp. 213-216, 266-283.

INTRODUCTION   25

stand why Rabelais turned to it to provide himself with the conceptualization of a dilemma that he perceived both as a creative writer and as a thinker. It is primarily the theory of Idea that will be considered, and the relation of language to Idea, for as Pantagruel's speech (pp. 22-23) indicates, this is the philosophic ground of the quest.

III

There is much truth in the spirit, if not the letter, of Plato's *doctrine es parolles* as Pantagruel cites it, for Plato's attitude toward language in relation to Idea, its function in the process of knowledge, is distinctly ambiguous.[17] At times, he says that words can adumbrate truth and that they serve as vehicles of instruction.[18] It is evident from his use of dialogue that he considers the spoken word the best method of teaching and evoking truth and he confirms this preference in the *Phaedrus* (275d-77b, 278b). Nonetheless, in the *Timaeus* (29b-c), he says that words are temporal entities perceived with the senses and hence epistemological underlings that can be relegated to the category of probability and opinion.

However, the best sense of Plato's ambivalence comes not from extrapolating statements from several dialogues, but from examining the dialogue which is entirely devoted to the language problem, the *Cratylus*.[19] Here Socrates mediates between two speakers holding

---

However, recent critics have returned to LeFranc's position to argue as unequivocally and as persuasively as he did so many years ago that Rabelais's books are indeed deeply penetrated with Platonic thought. See: G. Mallary Masters, *Rabelaisian Dialectic and the Platonic-Hermetic Tradition* (Albany: State Univ. of New York Press, 1969) and "The Hermetic and Platonic Tradition and Rabelais's *Dive Bouteille*," *Studi Francesi*, 10 (1966), 15-29. See also Florence Weinberg, *The Wine and the Will* (Detroit: Wayne State Univ. Press, 1972).

[17] The discussion of Plato's philosophy of language is based on two exigeses of the *Cratylus*: Marcia Colish, *The Mirror of Language: A Study in the Medieval Theory of Knowledge* (New Haven and London: Yale Univ. Press, 1968), pp. 9-10; and Ernst Cassirer, *The Philosophy of Symbolic Forms, I, Language*, tr. by Ralph Manheim (New Haven: Yale Univ. Press, 1953), pp. 117-126.

[18] See, in particular, *Gorgias*, passim, and especially 456b-58b, 464c-65e, 523b-27e; *Phaedrus*, 275d-79b.

[19] Rabelais knew the *Cratylus* well, if the testimony of his characters may be believed. In the *Quart Livre*, chapter thirty-seven, Pantagruel insists that

opposed and mutually exclusive positions. Cratylus argues that words refer naturally and necessarily to realities. Names, he says, have by nature a truth. If they did not, it would be impossible to make true statements (391b ff., 428e, 435d-38d). Hermogenes, to the contrary, argues that if words were necessarily true, it would be impossible to make false statements, and false statements can obviously be made. The relationship between words and realities, he maintains, is not logical. Words are arbitrary and purely conventional (429b ff).

Socrates takes up, one after another, the two terms of this paradox, but he does not resolve the controversy. To the contrary, he deepens it. In the beginning, we assume him to favor Cratylus' position, for he painstakingly tears down Hermogenes' argument and leads him to observe that words do have a logical relationship to reality, as revealed by the study of etymology and verbal classification. But these etymologies prove to be a double-edged sword — while they initially seem to substantiate Socrates' argumentation, they end up by undermining it. By their number, the increased speed and facility with which they are accomplished, the etymologies become a parody of themselves, a *reductio ad absurdum* of the very principle they set out to prove. And so, when he turns to Cratylus, Socrates has worked himself into a state of doubt that words do bear such a strict relationship to reality. In his second argument, he sets out to delineate the cognitive limitations of words.

With a nod in the direction of Hermogenes, he induces Cratylus to admit that convention does, in fact, play its part in the meaningfulness of words (434d-35b). But the thrust of his argumentation is larger than this. Socrates seems intent on situating the sphere of language at some midpoint between the realm of sensible realities and the realm of eternal truths. Language both reaches down to lower existences and strives upward toward higher ones, but by its very nature can never perfectly seize either, for the boundaries of the word are fluid. And herein lies Cratylus' error (and the one that Socrates committed with his etymologies) — that of deducing too strict a correlation between words and things, whether temporal

---

the names of the captains Riflandouille et Tailleboudin forecast a victory in the impending battle with the Andouilles: "Voyez le *Cratyle* du divin Platon. —Par ma soif, dist Rhizotome, je le veulx lire: je vous oy souvent le alleguant."

or supernal. Words are but imitations of reality, images — by definition one step removed from their referents. They cannot express them perfectly, if they could they would be identical with their referents and no longer images (432b, 439c-40d).

This inaccuracy is not so problematic in the case of words that refer to temporal realities, for we may "correct" the image by comparing it with the thing itself. But we have no objective referent for words that refer to atemporal, abstract realities. How then may we judge the correctness of these words? Fortunately, Socrates says, we possess an innate, transverbal criterion of truth (438d-439b), an observation which suggests that changeless realities can be known without the benefit of verbal intermediaries. This direct knowledge is preferable to the imperfect knowledge that language offers. Words are transient, but the soul and the objects of knowledge, the ideal forms, are eternal. Socrates' final injunction is that no man of sense should put the education of his mind in the power of names, for to do so is to condemn himself and other existences to what he calls "an unhealthy state of irreality" (440c). [20]

---

[20] We consulted the Jowett translation of the *Cratylus*, published in: *The Collected Dialogues of Plato including the Letters*, ed. by Edith Hamilton and Huntington Cairns (New York: Pantheon Books, 1961), pp. 421-474.

The *Seventh Letter* argues very much along the lines of Socrates' second debate in the *Cratylus*, a fact which Cassirer (*Philosophy of Symbolic Forms*, I, *Language*, p. 123) says is the strongest argument for the authenticity of the epistle. Here Plato talks at length about the imperfection of four things — names, descriptions, bodily forms and concepts — in relation to Idea:

> Names, I maintain, are in no case stable.... The same thing for that matter is true of a description, since it consists of nouns and verbal expressions, so that in a description there is nowhere any sure ground that is sure enough. One might, however, speak forever of the inaccurate character of each of the four! The important thing is that... there are two things, the essential reality and the particular quality, and when the mind is in quest of knowledge not of the particular but of the essential, each of the four confronts the mind with the unsought particular, whether in verbal or in bodily form. (*Epistles* 7.343 b, c, tr. by L. A. Post in *The Collected Dialogues of Plato*, p. 1950.)

As in the *Cratylus*, Plato stresses the transverbal criterion of truth. He says that the necessary attribute of one who seeks knowledge of the essential is an inborn affinity with it. For those who have none, knowledge of the four is useless. For those who have this inborn affinity, the four will only serve to bring them to the threshold of truth, where a silent and sudden flash of understanding will overwhelm them (344b, c).

The *Cratylus*, in its structure (and even in its themes), is not unlike Rabelais's prologue to *Gargantua* — both confront the reader with the problem of choosing between two arguments of equal force and plausibility. In the case of the *Cratylus*, it has been traditional to assume that Socrates' first argument is more characteristic of Plato's thought. However, it is his second statement, the notion of the "ineffability of truth," of the incapacity of language to express the Realities, rather than the "proper-name" theory which is dominant in the thought of the disciples of Plato in the succeeding centuries. From Plotinus,[21] through Proclus, Iamblichus and Dionysius the Aeropagite, there is the whole tradition of the *theologia negativa*, the impossibility of forming rational concepts of the Divine and of attaining the One by pure reason.[22] The concommitant of the *theologia negativa* is an ambivalent attitude toward language that was felt, with some justification, to be derived from Plato. On one hand, language was thought to be error and illusion, a veil hiding truth, self-deception. On the other, it was accepted as a necessary medium by which the way to truth may be taught and transmitted. Even if words were to be rejected once stated, they had first to be stated as an "aid to inquiry" (See n. 21). And so, the burden which the esoteric tradition put on language was that it had to transcend itself. Language had somehow to express the inexpressible. Speech had to point the way to silence.

This dilemma was solved as well as it could ever be solved by what Pico called "poetic theology"[23] — the notion of the veiling of

---

[21] See, for example, *Enneads*, V.5.6:

> Its definition (of the One), in fact, could only be "the indefinable".... We are in agony for a true expression; we are talking of the untellable; we name, only to indicate for our own use as best we may.... If we are led to think positively of the One, name and thing, there would be more truth in silence. The designation, a mere aid to inquiry, was never intended for more than a preliminary affirmation of absolute simplicity to be followed by the rejection of even that statement; it was the best that offered, but remains inadequate to express the nature indicated.

(tr. by Stephen Mackenna, *The Library of Philosophical Translations* [London: The Medici Society, 1926], IV, pp. 54-55.)

[22] See: Raymond Klibansky, *The Continuity of the Platonic Tradition during the Middle Ages* (London: Warburg Institute, 1939), p. 25.

[23] *Poetica theologia* is the title of a book Pico planned to write. He describes it in his *Commentary on Benivieni's Canzone d'amore*.

truth in oblique symbols, myths, allegories meant to stimulate contemplation. But even used symbolically, words ran a poor second to the visual symbol in the Renaissance, whose effectiveness language sought to emulate.[24] The Neo-platonists took Egyptian hieroglyphs as the highest model of mystical expressivity. Plato's reverence for Egypt was noted, and Egypt was the central and most sacred place of the *prisca theologia*, the tradition by which Plato was interpreted in the Renaissance.[25] The chain of ancient thinkers in which they placed him was thought to go back to the very dawn of creation, to Adam, and to Moses who confided the mysteries revealed to him on Mt. Sinai to the Egyptian priests. And from these great teachers, the mysteries were transmitted through all the "ancient fathers": Zoroaster, Hermes, Orpheus, Pythagoras, Plato and on into the Christian Era. Thus were all the great philosophers and all the world's religions felt to participate in the same revelation as Christianity, for their apparent diversity vanished when read "hieroglyphically." The Renaissance Neoplatonists revered the Egyptian ciphers and tried to emulate them with their own images, and Rabelais expresses his reverence for hieroglyphs at some length twice in the four books (G, 9; QL, Briefve Dec.) And, as Pico spoke of the process of interpreting the ciphers, he used the bone-marrow imagery so familiar to readers of Rabelais. Pico said that the hiero-

---

[24] See: E. H. Gombrich, "Icones Symbolicae: The Visual Image in Neo-Platonic Thought," *Journal of the Warburg and Courtauld Institutes*, 11 (1948), 163-192; and "Botticelli's Mythologies: A Study in the Neoplatonic Symbolism of his Circle," *Journal of the Warburg and Courtauld Institutes*, 8 (1945), 7-60.
See also: Edgar Wind, *Pagan Mysteries in the Renaissance* (Harmondsworth, England: Penguin Books, 1967); Mario Praz, *Studies in Seventeenth-Century Imagery* (Rome: Edizioni di Storia e Letteratura, 1964), second ed.; Robert J. Clements, *Picta Poesis: Literary and Humanistic Theory in Renaissance Emblem Books* (Rome: Edizioni di Storia e Letteratura, 1960); Liselotte Dieckmann, *Hieroglyphics: The History of a Literary Symbol* (St. Louis: Washington Univ. Press, 1970) and Karl H. Dannenfeldt, "Egypt and Egyptian Antiquities in the Renaissance," *Studies in Philology*, 6 (1959), 7-27. See also: Karl-Ludwig Selig, "Emblem Literature: Directions in Recent Scholarship," *Yearbook of Comparative and General Literature*, 12 (1963), 36-41, for a good bibliography.

[25] "Historically, Plato was considered as deriving from Moses; teleologically, as leading up to the Christian revelation." Daniel P. Walker, "Orpheus the Theologian and Renaissance Platonists," *Journal of the Warburg and Courtauld Institutes*, 16 (1953), p. 120. On the *prisca theologia*, see also Gombrich, "Icones Symbolicae," esp. 168-170.

glyphs showed "... only the crust of the mysteries to the vulgar, while reserving the marrow of the true sense for higher and more perfect spirits." [26]

The extensive use of paradox, as well as of symbols, was also characteristic of the Renaissance Neo-platonists. To point to the power beyond the Intellect, contradictory attributes were used, thereby negating those traits which would render it finite. By uniting contrary attributes in dialectical juxtaposition, the "mysterious cipher which comprises the contraries as One" was hinted at, "the One beyond being, the absolutely unfamiliar for which there is no fitting image or name. [27] Perhaps the most skilled dialectician of the Renaissance was Nicholas de Cusa, who stressed the coincidence of opposites in the hidden God, and who called the state of darkness in which all the distinctions of logic vanish "learned ignorance." [28]

IV

François Rabelais was familiar with this tradition and whether or not he "believed" in it, it nonetheless provided him with the conceptualization of the dilemma which he persistently tries to resolve in his four books. Whenever the quest for truth, itself a Platonic preoccupation, is the dominant theme, the whole complex of Neo-platonic attitudes toward language emerges. There is the recurrent eulogy of silence and the criticism of language: "... car ler matieres sont tant ardues que les parolles humaines ne seroyent suffisantes à les expliquer..." (P, 18). There is the continual interest in combining speech with silence by using gesture and mime or symbols and hieroglyphs — a continual tantalizing chain of references to hidden, higher meanings, a marrow to be sucked dry only by those already initiated into the mysteries they conceal. There is the ubiquitous use of paradox and dialectic which confront the opposites in a way which shocks reason but which points to a high folly, a truth where the opposites meet and merge in an inex-

---

[26] Translated and quoted by Wind, *Pagan Mysteries*, p. 17.
[27] *Ibid.*, p. 206.
[28] *Of Learned Ignorance*, tr. by Germain Heron (Hew Haven: Yale Univ. Press, 1954.)

pressible whole. These are several of the components of Rabelais's negative attitude toward words in relation to the quest for the Word which show the influence of Neo-platonism on him and which have caused us to designate him as *Homo Logos*.

But Rabelais is always, fully, supremely, *homo logos,* too; the same designation is also meant to describe the contrary impulse in him, the voice which persistently ridicules these Platonic concerns. No one has ever loved the human word as much as Rabelais, no one has ever explored its powers so thoroughly, played with it so joyfully. And his allegiance to it is philosophic as well as creative. The truths of the philologist persist in his mind, and these truths are human — concrete and tangible. Only through the word can one know them, through the word-as-it-is, not as a symbolic configuration. To *homo logos,* language is all we know and all we need to know, the alpha and omega of the world.

These two contrary attitudes function in dynamic antithesis throughout Rabelais's four books, for he could never decide which word to believe in. He believed in them both, he loved them both and he pursued the logos in both its natural and its supernatural aspects.[29] It is the simultaneous existence of these two opposed impulses which generates the continual ambivalence surrounding the quest and surrounding verbal creation in Rabelais's world. We began with the meeting of Panurge and Pantagruel to show how inextricably bound together are Rabelais's positive and negative attitudes toward his enterprise.

But of the two attitudes, the Platonic "méfiance de la parole humaine" comes to dominate more and more as Rabelais's creative life advances, and his growing uneasiness about language generates the quest for the logos which is at stake in the *Tiers and the Quart Livres*. Bound into the writer's joy in his powers of creation is an increasing nostalgia for the Word which is beginning and end, "le

---

[29] Kelley (*Foundations,* pp. 61-62) suggests in the works of Budé an ambivalence similar to that which we find in Rabelais: "Much as he loved philology, Budé could not help wanting to transcend language and to pursue the logos in its supernatural form, to pass beyond the historical world and devote himself to the things of the spirit.... After 1520, this attitude was intensified by a growing consciousness of his own mortality and of the ephemeral nature of human life."

Mot de la Vie". From their first meeting, the problem which confronted Panurge and Pantagruel was language and they were impelled to set out in pursuit of the Word. We will, in the following pages, follow their sibylline adventure.

Chapter I

THE RHETORIC OF SILENCE

The pursuit of the Word implies a critique of words. Silence is felt by Rabelais's questers to be more appropriate to the nature of their concerns, but silence is useless to the one who does not already possess the knowledge he is seeking. The quest for truth implies asking questions about that which is beyond speech, questions which cannot be answered, but yet must somehow be answered to forward the quester on his way. Those in pursuit of truth in Rabelais's four books attempt to resolve this dilemma by forging what may be termed a "rhetoric of silence." This involves two contradictory approaches to the problem, each of which will be studied separately in this chapter. The first rhetoric of silence concentrates on turning away from language to alternate forms of communication. Rabelais's characters experiment with color symbolism,[1] codes,[2] numbers,[3] and with painting,[4] but it is most often pantomime to which they turn in an attempt to transcend the limits of language. The second rhetoric of silence involves the opposite process, turning back to language in an attempt to perfect it as an object of inquiry. This is the process of *symbolization*,[5] and it

---

[1] *Gargantua*, 9-10 ("Les Blasons"), *Quart Livre*, 1 ("Les symboles et couleurs des navires").
[2] *Pantagruel*, 24 ("Lettre d'une dame de Paris").
[3] *Tiers Livre*, 20 ("Nazdecabre"), *Quart Livre*, 37 ("Riflandouille et Tailleboudin").
[4] *Quart Livre*, 2 ("Medamothi").
[5] This word is used by Rabelais in the *Tiers Livre*, chapter 3: "Entre les elemens ne sera symbolisation, alternation, ne transmutation aulcune." In Marcel Françon, "A note on the word "symbolisation" in Rabelais's *Tiers*

represents an attempt to combine speech with silence in an image which says something and points beyond itself to that which it cannot say.

The quest for the Word is introduced in Rabelais's work in 1532 by the Englishman, Thaumaste (P, 18-20), who comes to consult with Pantagruel about "...aulcuns passages de philosophie, de geomantie et de caballe, desquelz je doubte et ne puis contenter mon esprit" (18). He insists that language is inadequate to the nature of these concerns and suggests an alternate form of communication, a rhetoric of silence, to embody and communicate the ineffable truth which he is seeking:

> Mais voicy la maniere comment j'entens que nous disputerons. Je ne veulx disputer *pro* et *contra*, comme font ces sotz sophistes de ceste ville et de ailleurs; semblablement, je ne veulx disputer en la maniere des academicques par declamation, ny aussi par nombres, comme faisoit Pythagoras et comme voulut faire Picus Mirandula à Romme; mais je veulx disputer par signes seulement, sans parler, car les matieres sont tant ardues que les parolles humaines ne seroyent suffisantes à les expliquer à mon plaisir. (P, 18.)

By his concern with secret truth, his distrust of discursive language and his attempt to forge a "surlangage de l'ineffable," [6] Thaumaste identifies himself as a Neo-platonist. From his first words to Pantagruel where he quoted Plato, [7] he had unmistakably put his quest in this context. As he cites examples of seekers after truth who, like himself, journeyed to see the sages in whom wisdom had established her temple, he mentions the voyages of both Plato and Pythagoras to Egypt (18). These references recall the tradition of

---

Livre," *Modern Language Review*, 55 (1960), 84-85, he states that the three words are almost synonymous if one remembers that the primitive sense of symbol is "to put together, to exchange."

We are using this word in the conventional sense. However, the conventional sense includes the primitive one that Françon delineates. A symbol puts two things together; it is a metaphor "from which the first term has been omitted." See: Cleanth Brooks and Robert Penn Warren, *Understanding Poetry* (New York: Holt, Rinehart & Winston, 1960), p. 556.

[6] A term used by Michel Beaujour, *Le Jeu de Rabelais* (Paris: Editions de l'Herne, 1969), p. 143.

[7] "Bien vray est il, ce dit Platon, prince des philosophes, que, si l'imaige de science et de sapience estoit corporelle et spectable es yeulx des humains, elle exciteroit tout le monde en admiration de soy..." (P, 18).

the *prisca theologia*[8] which held that both philosophers had journeyed to study there. Thaumaste's association of the occult sciences with "philosophie" in general and with Christianity in particular also recalls this tradition. [9]

Pantagruel shows himself to be, if not a Platonist, at least sensitive to their concerns. His understanding of Thaumaste's dilemma is revealed by the titles of the books which he studies to prepare for the debate, especially by those titles which are fictitious. He reads *De Inenarrabilibus*, "On the ineffable," by Plotinus. Plotinus, of course, never wrote anything of this title; it is significant that Rabelais chose this term to characterize the *Enneads*. He also mentions the unknown work of an unknown author, Ynarius, *Peri Aphaton*, "On inexpressible things", as well as a known treatise of Hipponax, *Peri Anecphoneton*, "On things about which one must be silent." These titles indicate that Pantagruel apprehends that the debate will deal with matters that cannot be expressed, matters to which silence is truest. And yet, he sympathizes with Thaumaste's desire to teach and to be taught and thus explores several of the means of giving silence a rhetoric which have been suggested by the sages: Beda, numbers and signs; Proclus, magic; Artemidorus, dreams; Anaxagoras, signs; and Philistion, pantomime. (P, 18.)

Pantagruel is largely sympathetic to Thaumaste. He is skeptical that Thaumaste will find what he is looking for. Truth, Pantagruel says, is at the bottom of a bottomless pit. (Thaumaste will later concur in this judgment by referring to his concerns as "problemes insolubles" [20].) Nonetheless, the giant praises Thaumaste as a great wise man, lauds his desire to search for "la verité seule", and approves of gesture and sign as a medium of discussion appropriate to the nature of the quest. (18) In fact, Pantagruel's respect and sympathy for Thaumaste are so marked that the episode cannot be comic as long as he is the protagonist. The substitution of Panurge for Pantagruel is necessary for the farcical "débat par signes" to take place. This change of character divides the episode into two

---

[8] See Introduction, pp. 28-30.
[9] "... c'est Monsieur Pantagruel, duquel la renommée me avoit icy attiré du fin fond de Angleterre pour conferer avecques luy des problemes insolubles, tant de magie, alchymie, de caballe, de geomantie, de astrologie, que de philosophie, lesquelz je avoys en mon esprit." (P, 20)

parts which exhibit two distinct attitudes toward Thaumaste's quest and toward the language problem.

If chapter eighteen is generally sympathetic to Thaumaste and his Platonic concerns, chapters nineteen and twenty most assuredly ridicule them. It is at this point that Panurge steps in and the reversal of attitude takes place. The "débat par signes" (19) depends for its comic effect on the abrupt denigration of what Thaumaste and Pantagruel considered to be high and serious matters. The quest for the supra-real is ridiculed in the name of the physical and the palpable, for Panurge's gestures of derision almost all relate to urination, defecation and fornication. The comic also derives from Thaumaste's obvious blindness to the meaning of Panurge's gestures. Even after his defeat, when he "pissa vinaigre bien fort, et puoit comme tous les diables" (19), he remains unaware that Panurge has ridiculed him. As far as Thaumaste is concerned, he has dipped into "le vrays puys et abisme de encyclopedie" (20) and come up with the answers he wanted.

Thaumaste's mis-interpretation of Panurge's gestures explains why the quest for truth and the attempt to give silence a rhetoric always fail — because of that human frailty which Pantagruel will later call "philautie", self-love (TL, 29). Thaumaste is blind to all but what he wants to see, and gesture and mime serve his blindness as well as words. Pantomime, the means chosen to escape the limits of language, proves to be subject to the same limitations, for symbols, whether silent or verbal, are always interpreted subjectively. Thus, the rhetoric of silence and the quest for the absolute must inevitably end in the relative and are ridiculed for trying to transcend it.

But this does not nullify the sympathy for these concerns which Pantagruel expresses in the first part of this episode. Both his sympathy and Panurge's antipathy remain intact. Together the two parts of this episode express the ambivalence that characterized the meeting of Panurge and Pantagruel, that will characterize all of the episodes where truth and language are the dominant concerns. The quest is always both encouraged and ridiculed; language is always both praised and disdained. And the preference for silence is often expressed by the kind of joyous rhetoric which it is given in the "débat par signes."

The Thaumaste episode contains, in embryonic form, the structure and the main themes of the *Tiers Livre* and it is a fact of no little consequence that concerns which occupied Rabelais for only a few pages in 1532 become, in 1546, the matter of an entire book. The structure of the *Third Book* is similar to that of the Thaumaste episode — the man in quest of certainty who goes off to consult figures representative of all forms of wisdom, human and divine. Beginning with the dedication to Marguerite de Navarre, Panurge's quest is, like that of Thaumaste, put in a Neo-platonic context. It is concerned in part with the nature of women, the most popular aspect of Renaissance Platonism, but expresses more serious interest in the theory of Ideas, the cognate teachings of Reminiscence and the immortality of the soul, and in inspiration.[10] There is a general distrust of language in relation to the quest and a preference for silence. Many of the consultants in the *Tiers Livre* prefer, like Thaumaste, gesture and sign to speech. To begin with, Diogenes in the Prologue beats his tub "sans mot dire." La Sibylle de Panzoust relies mostly on gesture and sign, as do the fools Seigny Jean and Triboulet. And the outcome of these consultations is similar to that of Thaumaste with Panurge; the quester is ridiculed and gesture is proven to be as inadequate as speech to express an objective truth. One reverts to discursive language to interpret the symbols, and in so doing, finds that the symbols are open to more than one verbal interpretation. The circle is, in the deepest sense, a vicious one.

The *Tiers Livre* contains a second "débat par signes" which takes place between Panurge and the deaf-mute, Nazdecabre (19-20). This episode is a further development of the specific considerations which were raised in the Thaumaste episode. It, too, is enshrouded in the same ambiguity of attitude toward language — an initial serious approach to the language problem and a preference for silence are followed by a broadly comic, mimed "discussion" where these concerns are ridiculed.

---

[10] As we have argued in our Introduction, the theory of Ideas is the main background for the quest for truth. Interest is also expressed in the theory of Reminiscence in the chapter on dreams (TL, 13); on dying men as prophets (21); and in the consultation with Nazdecabre (19-20). The idea of divine furor, of inspiration, is discussed in the prologues to *Gargantua* and to the *Tiers Livre*, as well as throughout the *Third* and *Fourth* Books. See, *passim*, our chapters three, four and five.

In the first chapter of this episode (19), Pantagruel sets forth the arguments against the use of language and for a silent consultation with the deaf-mute, arguments which expand the considerations raised by himself and Thaumaste in the first book. Pantagruel argues first that language is by its very nature faulty and prone to mis-interpretation, that in antiquity, errors were made when consulting the oracles "...tant à cause des amphibologies, equivocques et obscuritez des motz, que de la briefveté des sentences.... Ceulx que l'on exposoit par gestes et par signes estoient les plus veritables et certains estimez." Thus he says that they should consult a mute who would be constrained to advise them "par signes sans parler" (19).

Pantagruel's insistence on the superiority of gesture to speech is preliminary to a discussion with Panurge on natural language. Panurge wonders if Pantagruel might be wrong in inferring that no speech is natural. When he says that, if it is true that no man speaks who has not heard speech, he could lead Pantagruel to "...logicalement inferer une proposition bien abhorrente et paradoxe" (19), he means that *someone* in the beginning had to have spoken without hearing language; else there would be no speech. Panurge may also have infantile speech in mind, for he offers as possible proof of "natural language" the experiment of Psammeticus, king of Egypt, who carefully secluded two children so that they did not hear speech of any kind. When released from this perpetual silence, they subsequently pronounced the Phrygian word *becus* which means "bread."

Pantagruel vehemently denounces this argument and states emphatically that no speech is natural:

> C'est abus, dire que ayons languaige naturel. Les languaiges sont par institutions arbitraires et convenences des peuples; les voix (comme disent les dialecticiens), ne signifient naturellement, mais à plaisir.

The only means of communication which is not arbitrary and purely conventional, he insists, is gesture.

However, not all gesture is natural. Pantagruel's subsequent examples play on the distinction between mime as a "universal" and as a "natural" language. He cites the examples of two mimics who once knew how to talk: Nello de Gabrielis who became deaf late in life, and the "joueur de farces" whom the King of Armenia chose above all else as a gift from Nero, for with the actor he could communicate with all the nations under his dominion. These two men illustrate the universality of gesture and sign. Nonetheless, because they once knew speech, their gestures are not natural, but "faincts, fardez, (et) affectez." Only the mime of one who has never heard speech constitutes a natural language. It is for this reason that Pantagruel insists that the consultant be not only mute but congenitally deaf, "sourd de nature," for only the gestures of this man will be "naifvement propheticques" (TL, 19).

This praise of deafness adds an important new dimension to the critique of language. Thaumaste had criticized language only as an *impediment* to the expression of truth, as "insufficient" for these arduous matters. Pantagruel's critique is more serious. He damns language as *corrupting* the innate knowledge of truth that we are born with. This recalls Plato's theory of Reminiscence, but Plato never suggested that it was human speech which obscured our memory of the Ideas. Rabelais gets the negative attitude toward language from the Neo-platonists who held that speech, evolved from and adapted to the objects of sensual perception, constitutes by its nature a barrier between man and the Supernal. The One can only be apprehended intuitively and in silence.[11] But Pantagruel's position is even more radical than the Neo-platonic one. He is suggesting that the knowledge of speech might impede even the silent intuition they so cherished. He is suggesting that language forms the mind and limits its scope — forms the mind so that it can intuit only the concepts and dimensions from whence language derives.

These high philosophic, hermetic considerations lead to the "débat par signes" where they suffer the same denigration as they did in the Thaumaste episode. The vulgarity of the episode in the *Pantagruel* is not as developed in the consultation with Nazdecabre. It is largely confined to Panurge's dissertation against a woman consultant, when he cites the examples of the Roman Verona and Soeur Fessue (19) to prove that women interpret all gestures venally. Nazdecabre's gestures are not particularly vulgar. In many cases, they are the actual symbols employed by antiquity to indicate

---

[11]-See our Introduction, pp. 28-30 and n. 21.

numbers and the meaning expressed by numbers.[12] The comic of chapter twenty rather derives from the rhetoric of silence — the gestures with which Panurge asks his questions and those with which Nazdecabre declares that he is doomed to be "coqu, battu, et desrobbé." It depends, too, on Panurge's "philautie." Pantagruel interprets Nazdecabre's gestures, and Panurge is joyful when they accord with his desires and stubbornly resistant when they do not. He persists in interpreting the mime to suit his own ideas, and the mental and verbal gymnastics necessary to do so are hilarious.

Panurge's blindness provides the moral of the "débat par signes" with Nazdecabre as well as the comic, and the moral is the same as that of the Thaumaste episode. Whether words or gesture or event, we interpret all phenomena to accord with our own desires. The limits of language reflect the limits that our nature and our condition as human beings impose on us — limits which we cannot escape. The attempt to transcend these limits by turning away from speech to gesture and sign is thus doomed to failure. The quester is ridiculed and the joy of human speech is always reaffirmed.

Whereas the first rhetoric of silence involves rejecting language in favor of alternate means of communication, the second rhetoric of silence turns back to it in an attempt to forge a language adequate to the concerns of the quester. This process has two stages. The first involves conferring "proper names" which express the essence of the designee. The second is more difficult, for it involves bringing a complex of attributes to bear on a name or an image. We call this the process of "symbolization." Four episodes are devoted to these related problems: "Les couleurs et livrée de Gargantua" (G, 9-10); "Le Pantagruélion" (TL, 49-52); "L'Isle des Alliances" (QL, 9); and "Riflandouille et Tailleboudin" (QL, 37).

In Plato's *Cratylus*, the subject under discussion is whether or not names signify by nature, by virtue of some intrinsic appropriate-

---

[12] The work of Beda alluded to in the Thaumaste episode, *De computo seu loquela per gestum digitorum* (called *De Numeris et Signis* by Rabelais) is generally considered as the original source for Rabelais in this chapter, although he might have read of number symbolism expressed by gestures in either Martianus Capella or in Agrippa's *De occulta philosophia*. See: Rabelais, *Tiers Livre*, ed. by Abel Lefranc *et al.*, IV, p. 154, n. 7. See also: W. F. Smith, "Rabelais on Language by Sign," *Modern Language Review*, 8 (1913), 196.

ness of the sign to the thing signified. Hermogenes argues very convincingly that they do not, that names are arbitrary, that there is nothing to prevent us from calling a horse a man (or vice versa), should we so desire (385a). Socrates agrees that we have this power, but he insists that we should not use it. A name, he says, is an instrument of teaching and distinguishing natures (385c) and therefore, "...(t)his giving of names can be no such light matter as you fancy or the work of light or chance persons... not every man is an artificer of names, but only he who looks to the name which each thing by nature has." (390 d, e). [13]

Rabelais is well aware of his power to do as Hermogenes suggests, but he is also aware of the responsibility that Socrates places upon him to be a good legislator of names. There is a recurrent attempt in these four books to forge "proper names", to make the designation reflect the nature of the designee. One thinks first of the names of his characters: Pantagruel, Panurge, Ponocrates, Epistemon, Xenomanes... all these are "proper names" which express the essence of the character. Rabelais even allows us once to be present at the naming ceremony. In the *Quart Livre,* chapter thirty-seven, the captains Riflandouille and Tailleboudin are chosen to lead the battle, for it is the essence of one to "rifler Andouilles" and of the other, to "tailler boudins". The *Cratylus* is specifically mentioned as the group pauses to discuss the relation of the names of these captains to the outcome of the impending battle with the Andouilles. [14]

The relation of name to thing is also the subject of an earlier episode in the *Quart Livre,* "Comment Pantagruel arriva en l'isle Ennasin et des estranges alliances du pays." (9.) However, the Ennasins bear "improper names." These are unattractive creatures whose odd names forge strange kinships between them. People-to-people relationships are mixed — an old man, for example, calls a little girl "my father", and she in turn calls him "my daughter." People-to-object relationships are also mixed in a long series of puns which ends with the marriage of a pear and a cheese.

---

[13] Plato, *Cratylus,* tr. by B. Jowett in *The Collected Dialogues of Plato,* pp. 423-429.

[14] "Voyez *le Cratyle* du divin Platon.—Par ma soif, dist Rhizotome, je le veulx lire: je vous oy souvent le alleguant. See our introduction, pp. 25-27.

Michel Beaujour has discussed this episode as a radical demonstration of the proposition that literary creation is in essence verbal *creation*; it is not an *imitation* of "reality" or "truth". [15] It imitates only sentences, descriptions, judgments of reality, but never reality itself. In literature, there is no difference between a unicorn and a horse, since both animals can serve as the subject of a sentence. [16] There is also no reason why the writer cannot designate children as fathers and fathers, children. The writer can manipulate words as he pleases and in so doing, he creates new worlds and new monsters which have a powerful verbal existence and which mock our fixed notions of reality. By "marrying" these creatures, Rabelais has found an apt image for the autonomy of verbal creations, their capacity to grow and change and engender new words and new beings, much as the first "alliances" which confronted the group inspired them to create dozens and dozens of new puns, new metaphors, new "alliances". The phenomenon of the Ennasins represents, as Beaujour suggests, "une prise de conscience des pouvoirs propres à la littérature, foncièrement menteuse et invétérée créatrice de fictions." [17]

There is much truth in what Beaujour says. Nonetheless, as difficult as it is to define, there always remains some standard of appropriateness in our minds, some notion of Physis, of Nature, against which fictional names, relationships and events are measured. The creation of fiction's other world implies the existence of this one. Antiphysie is just that — anti-nature — she is defined by her opposite and criticized in terms of it. This "sense" of nature is present on the *Isle des Alliances* in the midst of the display of the power of anti-nature, and it generates the ambivalence of the episode. For if the Ennasins are attractive to the group, they are also called "mal plaisans Allanciers" (10). And they are unpleasant for the same reason that they are attractive, because their names are "improper". They violate nature by jumbling the natural categories of age and gender and species.

Nor does Beaujour take into account the fact that the most flagrant fictions are capable of expressing deep and serious truths.

---

[15] This is the thesis of chapter 7 in *Le Jeu de Rabelais*, pp. 131-141.
[16] *Ibid.*, p. 135.
[17] *Ibid.*, p. 138.

A unicorn may well serve to tell of the nature of horses, indeed of any living creature, as a myth, a symbol. Rabelais, like so many of his contemporaries, shows a strong interest in symbolic language and there is a recurrent attempt in these four books to use words in this way. His symbols combine silence with speech in a verbal image which hints at nature's truths, hints at that which he cannot, or does not choose to, say directly.

Rabelais's first extensive venture into symbolization occurs in *Gargantua,* chapters nine and ten, where Alcofribas dissertates on the symbolic value of the colors blue and white in order to prove that they are the appropriate colors for Gargantua's livery, emblems which reveal his essence.[18] Alcofribas' methods of assigning emblems in chapter ten are to be contrasted with those against whom he rails in chapter nine. He attacks there *le Blason des couleurs* whose color symbolism is arbitrary. He also attacks the "transporteurs de noms" whose emblems, like those of the "mal plaisans Allanciers" are inauthentic, deriving from riddles and the play of sounds and not from an intrinsic relation between the symbol and the thing signified. Alcofribas criticizes these false symbols by holding them up to the emblems that he himself tries to emulate:

> Bien aultrement faisoient en temps jadis les saiges de Egypte, quand ilz escripvoient par lettres qu'ilz appelloient hieroglyphiques, lesquelles nul n'entendoit qui n'entendist et un chascun entendoit qui entendist la vertu, proprieté et nature des choses par icelles figurées; desquelles Orus Apollon a en grec composé deux livres, et Polyphile au *Songe d'Amours* en a davantaige exposé. En France vous en avez quelque transon en la devise de Monsieur l'Admiral laquelle premier porta Octavian Auguste. (G, 9)

We know of the deep reverence of the Renaissance Neoplatonists for the Egyptian ciphers as veiling the deepest truths of Nature and of the Divine,[19] and it seems certain from this passage that Rabelais

---

[18] For detailed analyses of the symbolism of this episode, See: M. A. Screech, "Emblems and Colours: The Controversy over Gargantua's Colours and Devices," *Mélanges d'histoire offerts à Henri Meylan* (Geneva: Droz, 1970), pp. 65-80; and G. Mallary Masters, "Rabelais and Renaissance Figure Poems," *Etudes Rabelaisiennes,* 8 (1969), 60-63.

[19] See our Introduction, pp. 28-30; and the bibliography suggested in notes 24 and 25.

shared their reverence. Morever, his fascination with hieroglyphs never waned. More than fifteen years later in the *Quart Livre,* hieroglyphs are found inscribed on the temples of "L'Isle des Macraeons" (QL, 25), and in the "Briefve Declaration" Rabelais praises them exactly as he does in the passage cited from the *Gargantua,* as models of symbolic language: "sacres sculptures... faictes des images diverses de arbres, herbes, animaulx, poissons, oiseaulx, instrumens, par la nature et office desquelz estoit representé ce qu'ilz vouloient désigner." Here, too, the great emblem books of the time are cited, the Horapollo,[20] the *Hypnerotomachia,* and the *Emblemata* of Andrea Alciati may also be alluded to.[21] And again in 1552, one special hieroglyph is singled out for particular praise:

> ... la divise de mon seigneur l'Admiral en une ancre, instrument tres poisant, et un daulphin, poisson legier sus tous animaulx du monde: laquelle aussi avoit porté Octavian Auguste, voulant designer: *Haste toy lentement; fays diligence parasseuse;* c'est à dire, expedie, rien ne laissant du necessaire.

Festina lente was praised by many humanists as the highest example of hieroglyphic wisdom, but Erasmus' adage was the most

---

[20] *The Hieroglyphics of Horapollo Niliacus, written by him in the Egyptian Tongue and put into Greek by Philip.* Nothing is known of either the author or the translator, and even the date of the work is uncertain. It was discovered in 1419 on the Island of Andros and brought to Florence. It was written in Greek, but translated into Latin during the Renaissance. The first Latin version was published by Aldus in 1505. See the English translation by George Boas (New York: Pantheon Books, 1950), which also has a good general introduction on hieroglyphs. See also, Liselotte Dieckmann, *Hieroglyphics,* pp. 26-30.

[21] Alciati's was the most important emblem book of the Renaissance, but we cannot simply assume its influence on Rabelais since the *Emblemata* was not published in France until 1534, the year the *Gargantua* appeared. However, Michael Screech ("Emblems and Colours") argues persuasively that the Augsberg edition of 1531 had swept through court circles and that Rabelais would surely have had access to this important work.

In a more specific vein, Screech connects the *Emblemata* to the allusion to "Monsieur l'Admiral" whom he identifies as Phillppe Chabot rather than Guillaume Gouffier, the traditional attribution. Chabot became admiral in 1536 and thus inherited the dolphin-anchor device which came with the post. This new identification is crucial to Screech's argument because Chabot was closely associated to the *Emblemata.* He was the patron of its publication in Paris in 1534, and a French translation, published in 1549, is dedicated to Phillippe Chabot. ("Emblems and Colours, esp. 65-67.)

influential praise and both of Rabelais's discussions reflect his reading of the great humanist. Not only is Rabelais's exposition of the motto similar, but his general remarks harken to the digression on hieroglyphs in the adage. Erasmus had stipulated, and Rabelais repeats, that the content of the emblems was not meant to be accessible to the vulgar — "nul n'entendoit qui n'entendist". "But if anyone deeply studied the qualities of each creature, he would at length, by comparing and guessing what they symbolized, understand the meaning of the riddles." [22] "Chascun entendoit qui entendist la vertu, proprieté et nature des choses par icelles figurées," in Rabelais's words.

But therein lies the rub of the hieroglyphic imagery which Erasmus admires and which Rabelais tries to emulate in forging his symbols: the understanding of a hieroglyph depends on prior understanding and on discursive reasoning. To explain the anatomy of emblems and how reason and intuition are combined in them, Wind uses Nicolas de Cusa's crucial paradox to say that they represent an intermediate state between *explicatio* below and *complicatio* above. [23] By *explicatio* is meant that the various elements of the symbolic configuration can be separated and simplified and examined by discursive knowledge. This process of "unfolding" is essential to the understanding of an image, but the more an image is "unfolded" and its parts analyzed, the farther it becomes removed from its essential meaning. This is acquired by means of the opposite process, "infolding," *complicatio* which, when it is complete, points to that which is beyond words. As Wind suggests, "Unless one knows what a hieroglyph means, one cannot *see* what it says. But

---

[22] Margaret Mann Phillips, *The Adages of Erasmus: A Study with Translations* (Cambridge, Eng.: The University Press, 1964), p. 175. The adage, *Festina Lente*, is found on pp. 171-190.

[23] *Pagan Mysteries*, pp. 204-205. Cusanus developed the antithesis *complicatio/explicatio* in his first philosophical work, *De docta ignorantia*, and as Ernst Cassirer says, it is a principle fundamental to his thought: "We can apply to Cusanus' thought the antithesis *complicatio and explicatio*, which he uses to illuminate the relationship of God to the world and of the world to the human mind. His thought blossoms out of *one* intellectual seed that progressively unfolds, and in this process of unfolding, absorbs the entire range and the entire *Problematik* of knowledge in the Quattrocento." *The Individual and the Cosmos*, tr. by Mario Domandi (New York; Barnes & Noble, 1963), p. 7.

once one has acquired the relevant knowledge, "unfolded" by more or less exoteric instruction, one can take pleasure in finding it "infolded" in an esoteric image or sign." [24]

As Erasmus "unfolded" the dolphin around the anchor, so does Rabelais engage, in chapter ten of the *Gargantua*, in extensive *explicatio* of his color symbolism. His purpose is double: to criticize the false symbols of the "transporteurs de nom" and of the *Blason des couleurs*, and to illustrate how a proper emblem is forged and interpreted. He calls on scriptural authority to prove that white symbolizes joy and pleasure. [25] He also, like Erasmus, relies on universal reason and the methods of Aristotelian logic. His *explicatio* of white makes it a successful emblem, for Rabelais is very careful to explain just how and why this color expresses "la vertu, proprieté et nature" of Gargantua.

However, no explication of the color blue is offered and it is mentioned only in passing at the end of chapter ten. [26] Its treatment is, in fact, so summary that one can only think back to the arbitrary color symbolism of the *Blason des couleurs*. One can also think ahead — to the final chapters of the *Tiers Livre* which comprise the eulogy of the plant known as "Pantagruélion". As with the color blue, Rabelais fails to give the exoteric instruction necessary to understand the deep meaning of Pantagruel's emblem. Here again, Rabelais begins in such a logical way that we expect the symbolism to be clarified: the description of the plant (49) is followed by a treatise on the naming of plants (50), which underscores the arbitrary nature of names and their inadequacy. We are thereby prepared to accept the new, "proper" name he confers on the hemp and we

---

[24] *Pagan Mysteries*, p. 208.
[25] "... je vous pourrois renvoyer au livre de Laurens Valle contre Bartole; mais le tesmoignage evangelicque vous contentera: *Math. xvij*, est dict que, à la transfiguration de Nostre Seigneur, *vestimenta ejus facta sunt alba sicut lux*, ses vestemens feurent faictz blancs comme la lumiere..." (G, 10).
White as *light* is a reading based on the Greek text. Rabelais is attacking the ignorance of Bartolus and of the *Blason des couleurs*, whose reading, "white as *snow*" came from the Vulgate. See Screech, "Emblems and Colours," 73-80. See also n. 55, pp. 72-73 of Screech's critical edition of the *Gargantua*.
[26] "... et diray en un mot que le bleu signifie certainement le ciel et choses celestes, par mesmes symboles que le blanc signifioit joye et plaisir." (G, 10)

await his explanation, but it never comes. We are never told just how the name expresses "la vertu, proprieté et nature" of either the plant or of Pantagruel. Though generations of critics have offered many interesting interpretations of this episode, none has succeeded in synthesizing all of the attributes of the "Pantagruélion" into a coherent symbolism.[27] We lack Rabelais's *explicatio* which would permit us to be certain.

However, if the lack of explication condemns us to uncertainty, it also gives us a wondrous freedom to engage in the game of hieroglyphic speculation that Rabelais must have enjoyed himself. We will now play that game, *serio ludere*, and offer this conjecture: that the "Pantagruélion" is Rabelais's own emblem of *festina lente*. Rabelais's allusions to this motto in the *Gargantua* and the *Quart Livre* attest to a life-long admiration. And, though the dolphin-anchor was the most common emblem of *festina lente*, it was but one of many. Edgar Wind counts over eighty variations of this motto in the *Hypnerotomachia* alone.[28] All of the "images diverses" that Rabelais enumerates in the "Briefve Declaration": "arbres, herbes, animaulx, poissons, oiseaulx, instrumens" could be — and were — used to represent *festina lente*, and many of these categories are in fact assimilated into the eulogy of the "Pantagruélion."

It is as a plant that the "Pantagruélion" is most directly linked to *festina lente*, for the maxim has its deepest roots, literally and figuratively, in the phenomenon of growth and ripening.[29] Augustus' motto was introduced by Aulus Gellius in the *Attic Nights*, X, xi, a chapter where he discussed the meaning of the adverb *mature*.[30] As nature allows plants to slowly ripen so that they may burst forth with fruit and flowers, so does *festina lente*, Gellius says, advocate that men combine "the promptness of energy and the delay of care-

---

[27] For a summary of the interpretations, see V. L. Saulnier, "l'Enigme du Pantagruélion," *Etudes Rabelaisiennes*, 1 (1956), 48-72.

[28] *Pagan Mysteries*, p. 103.

[29] See the chapter devoted to *festina lente* in *Pagan Mysteries*, "Ripeness is all," pp. 97-112. Our interpretation of the "Pantagruélion" was inspired by Wind's comments.

[30] Aulus Gellius, *The Attic Nights*, tr. by John C. Rolf (Cambridge, Mass.: Harvard Univ. Press & London: Heinemann, 1960), II, pp. 239-241. Although Rabelais does not mention Gellius in the "Pantagruélion," his name does come up in chapter 10 of *Gargantua*. The *Attic Nights* is also referred to in G, 3.

fulness... (I)t is from these two opposite qualities that *maturitas* springs."[31] And Pliny, too, had suggested that men take the "ripening" as a model for their moral lives. He designated the mulberry as the "wisest of trees," for it shows prudence in being the last to bloom, but once begun, the budding "is completed in a single night with a veritable crackling."[32] The men of the Renaissance often turned to Pliny for emblems of *festina lente*,[33] and Rabelais, as we know, based his own eulogy of the "Pantagruélion" on him.

Rabelais combines in the "Pantagruélion" the attributes of two plants as Pliny had described them, flax (*linum*) and hemp (*cannabis*).[34] And, although both plants remain distinguishable from one another in the "Pantagruélion," they are at the same time fused around a single phenomenon, the "ripening" which is the fundamental association of *festina lente*. The first stage of Rabelais's eulogy (49) is to describe in detail and at some length the *maturitas* of the "Pantagruélion": its appearance, how, when and where it comes to flower. This is clearly a portrait of *cannabis*, which also contributes rope and its medicinal properties to Rabelais's plant. Nonetheless, the primary virtue of the "Pantagruélion" remains its magical effect on navigation and it was *linum*, according to Pliny, which set boats to sail, making the world smaller and bringing all nature under man's dominion. But these wonders astound Pliny less than this fact: that "(f)lax is a plant which is grown from a seed(!)...[35] How audacious is life... that out of so small a seed springs a means of carrying the whole world to and fro...."[36] This same exclamation is the underlying paradox of the episode of the "Pantagruélion" — that all of its varied and awesome powers come from a humble plant, itself sprung from a seed. The entire episode is a tribute to *maturitas*.

---

[31] *Ibid.*, p. 241.

[32] Pliny, *Natural History*, XVI, xli, tr. by H. Rackham (London: W. Heineman, 1945), IV, p. 455.

[33] The mulberry was taken as a device of *festina lente* by Ludovico il Moro, for it alluded to his name (the mulberry is *morus* in Latin). Wind, *Pagan Mysteries*, p. 112.

[34] Flax is treated by Pliny in Natural History, XIX, i-vi. Hemp is discussed in XIX, xvi, and in XX, xcvii, its medicinal properties are set forth.

[35] *Natural History*, XIX, i, p. 421.

[36] *Ibid.*, p. 423. It should be noted that Pliny, unlike Rabelais, did not approve of navigation. The full quote begins "How audacious is life *and how full of wickedness...*"

This praise of nature and the moral wisdom which men draw from her processes is the fundamental association of the "Pantagruélion" and provides, in our opinion, its basic meaning. However, this meaning is expanded and other values are added to it. For the episode moves on from the phenomenon of growth and ripening (49) to describe how the plant is "preparé et mis en oeuvre" (50), and in chapters fifty-one and fifty-two are enumerated the manifold powers of the plant *after* it has been processed. In these last chapters, *festina lente* functions primarily as a strategy of art and invention. What we are meant to admire here are the many ways that man may insert his own powers into nature and control the ripening for his own benefit — "à l'insigne profict de la vie humaine" (51), as Rabelais puts it.

When the many "admirables vertues" of the plant are scrutinized, we see that men use it in fundamentally two ways. On one hand, Rabelais enumerates the ways in which the plant *qua* plant is processed and converted into numerous other forms. On this level, Rabelais is still close to the spirit and often the letter of Pliny's descriptions of flax and hemp. The fibers of the plant are extracted and made into rope. They are also woven into cloth which is used to make clothing, or nets, or awnings for theatres (50). The plant may also be boiled, mashed or crushed to obtain its juices, and in each form it is a potent medicine (which may be the reason why Doctor Rabelais chose *cannabis* as the "Ur-Pantagruélion.")[37] The

---

[37] Rabelais's enumeration of the medicinal values of the "Pantagruélion" follows Pliny (XX, xcvii) almost *verbatim*. There is, however, one significant omission. Pliny contended that: "It's seed is said to make the genitals impotent." Rabelais attributes to the plant, by implication, the opposite function: "Sans elle, seroient... les lictz sans delices..." (51).

Most of the medicinal functions of *cannabis* which Pliny enumerates were still used as folk remedies in the Middle Ages and into the sixteenth century. (For an outline of the history of *cannabis* and its uses, see: Solomon H. Snyder, "What we Have forgotten about Pot — A Pharmacologist's History," *The New York Times Magazine*, Dec. 13, 1970.) Although there is no indication that *cannabis* was used as an intoxicant in the Western World before the nineteenth century, a physician would have known that it "raised the pulse and enlivened the spirits" (*ibid.*, p. 121). And *cannabis* causes thirst, as does the "Pantagruélion." It is interesting to speculate that the plant's intoxicant powers may have had something to do with Rabelais's choice of *cannabis* over others to be Pantagruel's emblem.

plant also seems to provide food,[38] and its association with agriculture returns the "Pantagruélion" very closely to the primitive value of *festina lente,* for the arts of planting and husbandry, as no others, explore and control the phenomenon of growth and ripening.

The second class of its "vertus," however, leaves Pliny far behind, for here the "Pantagruélion" provides not its material form, but rather its energy. What is more important, it provides the *principle* of its energy, for men have learned to emulate nature and to themselves harness her force in a small space so that it may burst forth when force is needed. The most wondrous "vertus" of the plant fall into this category: the mechanistic models — the printing press, windmills and above all, those curious ships which seem literally to fly over the ocean.[39] As these inventions are enumerated, the "Pantagruelion" seems to have left far behind the pastoral imagery which is its homeland. Yet these "technological" wonders also spring forth from a "seed," one which is man-made, but a seed nonetheless:

> Je diray plus. Icelle herbe moyenante, les substances invisibles visiblement sont arrestées, prinses detenues et comme en prison mises; à leur prinse et arrest sont les grosses et pesantes moles tournées agilement à l'insigne profict de la vie humaine. (51)

It is this seed which provides the energy to lift Rabelais's boats off the water and put them in flight. And with them, the episode leaves behind both past and present and is thrust into the future. The "Pantagruélion" is finally a vision. It is a Promethian vision, and we see the gods tremble as men implacably push toward Olympus to displace them. For *festina lente* is the deepest secret of nature's power, heretofore the secret of the gods, and men have seized it at last. Their future is one of limitless power and endless possibilities.

---

[38] "Sans elle, seroient les cuisines infames, les tables detestables.... Sans elle, ne porteroient les meusniers bled au moulin, n'en rapporteroient farine.... De quoy feroit on chassis?" (51)

[39] "Icelle moyenant, par la retention des flotz aërez sont les grosses orchades, les amples thalameges, les fors guallions, les naufz chiliandres et myriandres de leurs stations enlevées et poussées à l'arbitre de leur gouverneurs". (51).

Rabelais's association of mechanistic models to *festina lente* is not unusual; his contemporaries used devices such as the catapult, the cannonball, gunpowder, bellows and rockets as emblems of this maxim.[40] But we must not forget that, although they were certainly praising human invention, the men of the Renaissance were using these mechanistic models as *emblems,* as symbols of a perfection that was first and last moral and behavioral. Whether the symbols were taken from the natural world, or from "technology," they were employed to express the *maturitas* which Gellius praised as the highest wisdom, that wisdom which Erasmus defined as "a wise promptness together with moderation, tempered with both vigilance and gentleness...."[41] It is as a moral maxim that *festina lente* stands as the conclusion of the *Tiers Livre*. It affirms both voices of the dialectic of the book, affirms both Pantagruel's prudence and Panurge's blind "bursting forth," and it praises the union of opposites that their friendship represents. It is also as a moral maxim that the "Pantagruélion" stands as the prelude to the voyage of the *Quart Livre. Festina Lente* encourages that wise moderation which the author lauds in his prologue to this book, a virtue needed to survive the encounters with the intemperate monsters who inhabit Rabelais's comic Inferno. *Festina lente* is the light of Physis which shines in the darkness of Antiphysie. It is the one, all-embracing "idée et exemplaire de toute joyeuse perfection."

However, it must be admitted that this interpretation of the "Pantagruélion" must ultimately suffer the fate of the others. Too many things are left unexplained, especially by the last chapter of the episode where the powers of the "Pantagruélion asbestin" are described (52). This chapter brings into the foreground the dark

---

[40] Wind, *Pagan Mysteries,* pp. 108-111. Wind says that these mechanistic models belonged to a phase of the Renaissance imagination called *magia naturalis*. Natural magic was distinct from black magic by its enlightened methods of inquiry and by the fact that it was considered to be part of natural philosophy, its very summit, for natural magic was "natural philosophy in action." The natural magician was he who learned the proper inducements for revealing the latent forces of nature. By inserting his magic art into nature, he was able to release forces greater than his own. It was thus that gunpowder and the cannonball could be seen as models of moral virtue, for natural magic was seen as a moral force. It made man recognize in himself the forces of nature and in nature, a model of his own force. (*Ibid.,* 110-111).

[41] *Adages,* p. 172.

side of the "Pantagruélion" which has been latent throughout the episode: it "kills" as well as it cures, and it is associated with death and destruction, attack and besiegement in chapter fifty-two. The plant's dreadful side does not correspond to *festina lente*.

Therefore it must be said that whereas gesture and mime failed because one reverted to language and interpretation, the second rhetoric of silence fails for the opposite reason — the writer does not do enough interpretation. "Nul n'entendoit qui n'entendist...": because Rabelais himself does not give sufficient *explicatio*, all explications are unverifiable conjectures and the meaning of his hieroglyphs remains closed to us. Thus Rabelais's attempt to establish true relationships between name and thing results in a set of esoteric symbols which remain, after hundreds of attempts to decipher them, as enigmatic as ever. One way or another, Rabelais's language always eludes us. One wonders if it did not elude, always, the writer himself.

CHAPTER II

PARADOX AND THE CRITIQUE OF FICTION

Leo Spitzer commented once of Rabelais that he must have realized the paradox which haunted his whole artistic activity — that fiction creates *unreal reality* as does language in general.¹ We have discussed, in Chapter one, Rabelais's ambivalent attitude toward language *per se*. Now we will discuss his ambivalent attitude toward the specific use of language by the writer of fiction. In many episodes, particularly in the *Gargantua*, but also in the *Tiers Livre*, Rabelais uses paradox to make us aware of the paradox of fiction's unreal reality. By juxtaposing contradictory arguments, the writer displays his power to convince and to manipulate our credulity, and in so doing, he shocks us into a "critical realization of fiction's operation."²

It is, in Rabelais's work, the persona of Alcofribas Nasier who plays on the paradox of fiction's unreal reality and in so doing, simultaneously praises and derides fiction's power. Alcofribas himself embodies a paradox, that of inverted self-reference.³ François Rabelais writes himself into his book as Alcofribas Nasier who is both story-teller and a character in the story he is narrating — alternately a drunkard and a scholar-philosopher, *copain* and teacher, factotum, courtier, friend of princes and social critic. One of Alcofribas' most prestigious tricks, where self-reference is inverted so

---

¹ Leo Spitzer, "The Works of Rabelais," p. 144.
² Rosalie Colie, *Paradoxia Epidemica: The Renaissance Tradition of Paradox* (Princeton: Princeton University Press, 1966), p. 45. See the Introduction, pp. 3-40 for an excellent study of the dynamics of paradox, as well as the fine chapter on Rabelais, pp. 43-71.
³ *Ibid.*, pp. 69-70.

often that one is lost in its mazes, is the moment when he climbs onto the tongue of Pantagruel, descends into his throat, and returns six months later to recount the wonders of the world that *he* put into the mouth of the character that *he* created (P, 32). The ambiguities which can be brought to bear on the pronoun "he" resemble Eliot's "wilderness of mirrors"[4] — the world in Pantagruel's mouth is the world in Alcofribas' mouth which is the world in Rabelais's mouth which is something other than the world.[5]

The complex inversion and re-inversion of self-reference in this episode of the *Pantagruel* is only the most extreme display of the writer's power to jumble the categories and levels of the unreal reality he is positing. Alcofribas' whole essence is Protean. He plays and laughs, then stops to tell us to take him seriously, and we always suspect that he is either more or less serious than he is pretending to be. This "je" is, like the "I" who speaks in Erasmus' *Praise of Folly*, a point of view inherently suspect. The fictional Alcofribas informing us of his "tant veritable histoire" is, like folly praising folly or the Creton Epumenides saying that all Cretons are liars, "an insoluble dilemma of permanent uncertainty."[6]

His existence and his nature a paradox, Alcofribas systematically uses paradox to display the processes by which the writer convinces his audience of fiction's unreal reality. In the *Gargantua*, his paradoxes play on three different, but related issues. There are, first, the paradoxes which deal with the problem of interpretation; second, those which criticize authority; and third, the utopia-anti-utopia juxtapositions.

The pattern of all the book's paradoxes is established in the famous prologue to *Gargantua* where Alcofribas posits two equally convincing, but contradictory arguments side by side. The theme of both arguments is the meaning of the tale to follow — how to, or how not to, interpret Alcofribas' exposition of the giant's adventures. To develop this theme, both halves of the Prologue play on the

---

[4] T. S. Eliot, "Gerontion," in *The Waste Land and Other Poems* (New York: Harcourt, Brace and World, 1934), p. 21.

[5] We are, of course, re-phrasing the most felicitous title of Erich Auerbach's chapter on Rabelais, "The World in Pantagruel's Mouth" in *Mimesis*, tr. by Willard Trask (Garden City, N. J.: Doubleday Anchor Books, 1957), pp. 229-249.

[6] Kaiser, *Praisers of Folly*, p. 36.

appearance-reality paradox, but the arguments are reversed in midstream. Alcofribas first uses a sequence of images which were commonplace among the Neo-platonists of his time, the Socrates-silenus-marrowbone images, to convince his audience that his tale is more serious that it seems, that it contains hidden wisdom under its grotesque surface. The reader is exhorted to emulate Plato's philosophic dog and ignore the bone for the marrow: "... par curieuse leçon et meditation frequente, rompre l'os et sugcer la sustantificque mouelle — c'est à dire ce que j'entends par ces symboles Pythagoricques...." Then, in an abrupt *volte-face*, Alcofribas contradicts this exhortation almost point by point. He insists that he spent scarcely any time composing the book, and he warns any *glosateur de texte* against too much "curieuse leçon et meditation frequente" of his story. After convincing the reader that the appearance of the book belies its reality, he insists at the end that the appearance *is* the reality. The bone, he says, contains no marrow. These are not "symboles Pythagoricques," but empty words, "belles billes vezées."

The second and third interpretation paradoxes of the *Gargantua*, "Les Fanfreluches Antidotées" and "L'Enigme en Prophetie," stand at the beginning and the end of the narrative and by thus enclosing it, underscore how vital is the meaning problem posed *serio ludere* in the Prologue. The "Fanfreluches" bear the same relation to the Prologue as the "Enigme en Prophetie" does to the two interpretations offered by Gargantua and Frère Jean. This first poem offers the reader a text where the meaning problem posed by Alcofribas in the Prologue can be practically demonstrated. Are we to follow his first exhortation and dig for hidden meanings in the "Fanfreluches," for Pythagoric symbols concerning "nostre religion... l'estat politicq et vie oeconomicque"? Or are we to take the "Fanfreluches" for the nonsense they appear to be, following Alcofribas' second demand: "Tenez-moy tousjours joyeux"? No resolution of the dilemma, of course, is offered by the mystifying Alcofribas.

The "Enigme en Prophetie," found buried as were the "Fanfreluches," also tantalizes with the hint of hidden meanings. Gargantua emulates the "chien-philosophe" and ignores the bone for the marrow which he believes refers to the persecution of the Evangelicals. Frère Jean laughs at his master's allegories and interprets the poem as a description of a tennis game. As with the Prologue and the "Fanfreluches Antidotées," no choice can be made between the two interpretations of the "Enigme en Prophetie" because both are equally plausible, equally convincing, and mutually exclusive.

The meaning problem posed by these three paradoxes cannot be solved by choosing to believe only one-half of the two-pronged argument, for these paradoxes "mean" both of their terms, that the *Gargantua* is both more and less serious than it seems to be, that the enigmas and the book are offered *serio* as well as *ludere*. The problem of meaning is better approached by considering the function of paradox, which is to stimulate thought. By posing the problem of interpretation *serio ludere*, Alcofribas disallows his audience its usual function of passive "listener" or "reader". He does not simply state that meaning will be a problem, he confronts his readers with actual meaning problems, and one is forced to become a problem-solver, an active participant in the fiction and in the fiction-making.

By forcing the reader to think, these interpretation paradoxes simultaneously perform two contradictory functions. On one hand, they *involve* the reader in the fiction. Floyd Gray argues that this is so when he says that the ambiguity of the Prologue prepares for and embodies the nature of the fictional reality of the *Gargantua* where the reader must swing back and forth from the frankly fictional to the fictionally real, from the world of giants to the world of men.[7] Alcofribas' intention in juxtaposing contradictory propositions is to "involve and lose the reader in ...(the) shifting planes" of the fictional world he is positing.[8]

However, on the other hand, by stimulating thought, these paradoxes also perform the opposite function — of keeping the reader at a critical distance from the fiction. It is a technique not unlike that of Bertolt Brecht, who wilfully shatters the illusion of reality by displaying the theatrical rigging behind the dramas played on-stage.[9] Rabelais's flagrant display of his power to pull the strings of our credulity this way or that, like a puppet-master, for his own pleasure and to his own ends, shocks us into a critical realization

---

[7] Floyd Gray, "Ambiguity and Point of view in the Prologue to *Gargantua*," *Romanic Review*, 56 (1965), 12-21.

[8] *Ibid.*, 19.

[9] We are referring to *Verfremdungseffeckte* (alienation effects) which Martin Esslin defines as "... devices which would prevent identification to the point of annihilating the suspension of disbelief...." (*Bertolt Brecht* [New York and London: Columbia Univ. Press, 1969], p. 13.)

of fiction's power to create unreal worlds and convince us of their reality. He systematically jolts us out of the willing suspension of disbelief that fiction requires of us, into that state of awareness that Beaujour ascribes to the writer himself when he speaks of "une prise de conscience des pouvoirs propres à la littérature, foncièrement menteuse et invétérée créatrice de fictions." [10]

We are stimulated, too, to think beyond literature's unreal reality to consider the problem of fiction as it relates to what we call "reality". The anatomy of the Prologue and of the "Enigme en Prophetie," with the strict correspondence of opposites, mirrors the Januslike nature of all the world's phenomena. As Panurge will learn in the *Tiers Livre,* where the epistemological implications of the critique of fiction are more developed, at least two interpretations of any experiential or existential "fact" can be offered and logically substantiated. That it is possible to argue convincingly in favor of either of the opposites implies that our worlds, like the one which Alcofribas is presenting, are also verbal in substance. Truth, like literature, consists of numerous selected fictions, each of which is only convincing as long as it is not confronted with another fiction of equal persuasiveness.

Alcofribas' voice, although it permeates the entire *Gargantua,* is particularly dominant up to chapter eleven, "De l'adolescence de Gargantua." This chapter begins with the giant's name; it marks the point where Alcofribas' overt control wanes. Gargantua is now, so to speak, old enough to talk for himself. But up until that point, it is the opinionated and mystifying voice of Alcofribas which not only narrates events, but also comments on them and participates in them. As long as he is the main character, through chapter ten, he uses a type of paradox similar, but not identical, to that used in the Prologue and the two enigmas — what Tetel terms "la protestation de véracité". [11] These are paradoxes which throw into question less the interpretation of the story than the authority of the storyteller, as well as questioning the veracity of all established authorities. This type of paradox, the authority paradox, is used

---

[10] *Le Jeu de Rabelais,* p. 138.
[11] Marcel Tetel, *Etude sur le comique de Rabelais* (Florence: Leo S. Olschki, 1964), pp. 69-70.

in chapter three, "Comment Gargantua fut unze moys porté ou ventre de sa mere"; chapter six, "Comment Gargantua nasquit en façon bien estrange"; and in chapters nine and ten which discuss "Les couleurs et livrée de Gargantua."

Chapter six gives the anatomy of the authority paradox in its most complete form. It begins with first positing a fictional fact, the birth of Gargantua through his mother's left ear. This is accepted as "true" in the context of Alcofribas' fantastical world. Our expectation is that he will continue to elaborate, but instead the "je" intervenes to question our belief: "Je me doubte que ne croyez asseurement ceste estrange nativité. Si ne le croyez, je ne m'en soucie, mais un homme de bien, un homme de bon sens, croit tousjours ce qu'on luy dict et qu'il trouve par escript."

The next stage of the argument is to introduce authorities, ostensibly to substantiate his statements, but which actually undermine his own authority as well as the authorities which can be called on to support such a phenomenon. The authorities he uses are the highest and most respected. He alludes first to the Bible,[12] and then to six miraculous births recorded by classical writers, including the births of Rocquetaillade and Crocquemouche which are myths of his own making. These outrageous myths undermine simultaneously the authority of the classical writers, the authority of the scriptures, and the authority of Alcofribas himself. The effect of his "protestations de véracité" is to convince us of exactly the opposite of what he says he means to convince us — that a man of good sense does *not* believe everything he reads or is told.

The next twist in the argument brings it to its typical end "en queue de poisson." Alcofribas does not resolve the issues he has raised; he stimulates further thought by throwing the reader out of the fiction to think for himself about the issues he has raised:

> Mais vous seriez bien dadvantaige esbahys et estonnez si je vous expousoys presentement tout le chapite de Pline auquel parle des enfantemens estranges et contre nature;

---

[12] It is possible that this episode is a parody of the Virgin Birth, a miracle not mentioned by St. Paul, the favorite apostle of the Evangelicals. The Virgin Birth is mentioned only by Matthew (I:18-25) and Luke (I:30-35) and in the most oblique terms. Luke, for example, records: "And the angel answered and said unto her, The Holy Ghost shall come upon thee, and the power of the Highest shall overshadow thee..." (I:35).

et toutesfoys je ne suis poinct menteur tant asseuré comme il a esté. Lisez le septiesme de sa *Naturelle Histoire, capi. iij*, et ne m'en tabustez plus l'entendement.[13]

"Menteur" is the key word of this episode as it is of all the "protestations de véracité." What is at stake is the veracity of all authorities that are usually believed without qualification — the Bible, the classical writers, particularly Pliny in chapter six, whom Rabelais quotes so frequently throughout his book. But what is also at stake is the authority of Alcofribas. He throws into doubt his authority as an expositor of fictional "facts" and thereby breaks the illusion of reality which the writer of fiction more characteristically tries to create.

The "protestation de véracité" also constitutes the dynamism of chapters three and ten. In chapter three, he posits the fact that "Gargantua fut unze moys porté ou ventre de sa mere." Like the giant's birth, this is a statement before which we would willingly have suspended our disbelief had not Alcofribas called the machinery of the fiction to a halt to question our credulity. Here, too, he piles up a dozen authorities to substantiate the fiction, thereby casting suspicion on the authorities he cites as well as on his own authority. In chapter ten, Alcofribas argues eloquently that white signifies joy and pleasure, using the methods of Aristotelian logic, universal reason, and calling on authorities from the Bible and ancient thinkers. However, the entire edifice comes to rest on examples taken from the classics of people who died laughing, examples offered by the same writers — Aristotle, Pliny, Galen, etc. — who had supported his earlier contentions. Moreover, his summary treatment of the color blue recalls the arbitrariness of the color symbolism of *Le Blason des couleurs* whose very methods Alcofribas set out to criticize.[14] This facetious ending casts doubt on the authority of the ancients, as well as on Alcofribas' entire

---

[13] In Book VII, iii, Pliny is discussing the portentious power of strange and monstrous births. He lists, among others, multiple births exceeding triplets, animals — serpents and elephants (!) — born to women, and he ends with the amazing case of a baby who turned around and climbed back into the womb because the day he was to be born seemed inauspicious. *Natural History*, 2, pp. 527-528.

[14] See Chapter I, p. 46.

argument in chapter ten which, to this point, had seemed straight-forward.

These "protestations de véracité" have been studied as a comic technique in Rabelais's work.[15] They certainly do elicit laughter, but the laughter is not whole-hearted since they create, and depend on, uncertainty and confusion in the reader. The authority paradox may also be seen as a means of teaching the humanist point of view. By continually calling into question the established authorities, scriptural, classical and that of the ecclestical and scholarly hierarchs of his time, Rabelais is predicating the critical spirit which was so fundamental to humanism. No authority was to be accepted without examination — neither that of the commentators of the scriptures or of classical texts, nor the scriptural or classic texts themselves. Their authority was to be measured against reason and experience. "Un homme de bon sens," to rephrase Alcofribas' injunction, "*ne* croit *pas* tousjours ce qu'on luy dict et qu'il trouve par escript."

However, if Alcofribas is a humanist, he is also an "anti-novelist." If he is criticizing the authority of "les doctes," he is also calling attention to the spuriousness of his own authority. The "je" is a voice which we are taught to regard with a mixture of admiration and distrust, for he continually manipulates our belief in him, twisting his arguments to confuse our perspective. Beginnings, middles, and ends, right and wrong, up and down — this whirling dervish jumbles and commingles all the categories at will. He draws attention to the power of his artifice to remind us that literature is, like Alcofribas himself, "foncièrement menteuse."[16] The power of language and of fiction is a cause for rejoicing in the writer and his audience, but its dangers and limitations are persistently underscored.

Of all the critiques of fiction in Rabelais, the utopian theme plays most intensely on the paradox of fiction's unreal reality. For the anatomy of a utopia is exactly the same as the anatomy of

---

[15] This is Tetel's view (*Etude sur le comique*, pp. 69-70.) He does however underscore that the irony of this device tempers the comic: "... cette formule n'est qu'une feinte pour se jouer de nous. Elle correspond à une forme de charlatanisme qui est, d'ailleurs, le résultat naturel des hâbleries dans l'oeuvre rabelaisienne." (p. 69)

[16] Beaujour, p. 138.

fiction; both make "positive statements about a non-existent thing."[17] All utopias are fictional; they present the world with its imperfections removed. Thus, they constitute a criticism of human nature and human institutions. But because the utopian fiction, Antiphysie, is derived by reversing the "extant thing," Physis is present by her exclusion, as a foil against which the utopia is measured. And so, while the ideal critizes human nature and human institutions, the notion of Physis imposes itself to criticize the utopia for denying life-as-it-is. It is this dialectic between Physis and Antiphysie which constitutes the inherent dynamism of utopias.

Rabelais makes this dialectic explicit by using a technique similar to that of the Prologue and the "protestations de véracité." He juxtaposes next to a utopian construct, down-to-earth considerations drawn from a here-and-now which is much less gracious, thereby undermining both the fiction and the "reality" opposed to it. The Abbaye de Thélème, for example, is set up point by point "au contraire de toutes aultres." (G, 52.) Whereas other religious institutions constrain human nature, the Abbaye de Thélème offers total freedom: FAYS CE QUE VOULDRAS (G, 57), because man, uncorrupted by harsh and unnatural regimentation, is essentially good. However, embedded, significantly, in the very foundations of this utopia is the "Enigme en Prophetie" which refers to life as it is and men as they are. This panorama of strife and violence is offered immediately after the description of life in the Abbaye de Thélème to remind that in the "real world" there is war, not peace, and those "hypocrites, bigotz, matagotz" (G, 54) who were banished from Thélème are in actuality the governors of a world wherein the elegant goodness and simplicity of the *Thélèmites* is persecuted.

Picrochole, too, falls victim to the "real world" (G, 33). While his utopian fiction of conquering the world has none of the social and philosophic content of the Abbaye de Thélème, it has the same moral — that wishing, and recording the wish, does not make it so. As they weave a narrative of world conquest, Picrochole and his captains are both story-teller and audience, deceiver and deceived. The fiction they construct has nothing to do with the "reality" of Gargantua's superior force and strategy, and Picrochole's grandiose

---

[17] Colie, p. 52. For a discussion of utopias as paradoxes and of the Abbaye de Thélème, see, pp. 49-53.

dreams are followed immediately by events which lead to his ignominious defeat.

The *Tiers Livre* opens with a utopia - anti-utopia paradox which is complicated by the fact that it operates on two levels, a literal and a figurative one. In chapters three and four, Panurge sets forth his praise of borrowing and lending which presents a vision of universal love and charity not unlike the spirit of the Abbaye de Thélème. Insofar as "dettes" mean "dettes," it is a satirical eulogy — the praise of an unworthy thing.[18] But insofar as debts are a metaphor for *caritas,* he is serious. Panurge is, in the "éloge des dettes," simultaneously a hypocritical *blagueur* and a singer of World Harmony,[19] a n'er-do-well who makes a religion of debt-making and a preacher of the Pauline sentence of Gargantua's emblem: Charity seeketh not its own (G, 8). In Panurge's cosmology, all of the elements of both the macrocosm and the microcosm seek to contribute to the larger goal of maintaining universal life.

This utopia is confronted by two anti-utopian constructs. There is first, immediately following Panurge's eulogy of borrowing and lending, Pantagruel's praise of the self-contained man who borrows and lends only when his best efforts have been exhausted (5). The principle of individuation opposes the principle of involvement, but neither wins the argument — these two conflicting points of view each stand intact. Pantagruel, normally to masterful at straightening

---

[18] This is the thesis of C. A. Mayer, "Rabelais' Satirical Eulogy, the Praise of Borrowing and Lending," in *François Rabelais, Ouvrage publié pour le quatrième centenaire...,* pp. 147-155. See Leo Spitzer's critique of this article in "Rabelais et les rabelaisants," *Studi Francesi,* 4 (1960), 401-423.

Two other readings of the *éloge des dettes* might be mentioned here; that of Robert Marichal who sees it as a parody of the role assigned to love by Ficino ("Rabelais devant le Néoplatonisme," 185-187) and of G. Mallary Masters who sees Panurge's praise of debts as an ironic inversion of the harmony of the world (*Rabelaisian Dialectic,* pp. 24-27). It must be said, however, that Spitzer's work stands as a critique of Master's thesis. Spitzer was a student of World Harmony. See: *Classical and Christian Ideas of World Harmony: Prolegomena to an Interpretation of the Word 'Stimmung',* ed. by Anna Granville Hatcher (Baltimore: Johns Hopkins, 1963.) And Spitzer repeated many times that Panurge's arguments in the *éloge des dettes* do indeed relate to this concept. See, for example, "The Works of Rabelais," pp. 136-137; "Le prétendu réalisme," 147-148, *Linguistics and Literary History* (Princeton: Princeton Univ. Press, 1963), p. 18; as well as the rebuttal of Meyer's article, as cited above.

[19] Spitzer, "The Works of Rabelais," pp. 136-137.

out faulty reasoning, can find no flaw in Panurge's argumentation. The question is only settled by his exercise of the kingly prerogative of ordering his subject to be silent and obey. That is to say, it is not settled at all.

The second set of arguments against the utopian vision of the "éloge des dettes" is set forth by Panurge himself in chapter nine. The entire edifice of his *encomium* had come to rest on the idea of procreation, which put the "puce" in his "aureille" and caused him to think of marriage. And so, he cast aside all thoughts of war, adorned himself in the toga of peace, and prepared to engage in the search for a wife with whom he could live in the state of happy give-and-take he had envisioned in his utopia. However, the battle of the sexes is an inescapable fact of life. It is Panurge himself who, in chapter nine with the echo of Pantagruel, contrasts his own utopian vision of love and charity with the facts of marriage that he has observed — that women do cuckold and rob and even occasionally (at least in medieval literature) beat their husbands. Panurge is unable to decide either to marry or not to marry because the dialectic between his utopian ideal and grim reality is, as he puts it: "...la chanson de Ricochet. Ce ne sont que sarcasmes, mocqueries, et redictes contradictoires. Les unes detruisent les aultres. Je ne sçay es quelles me tenir" (TL, 10).

Abraham Keller makes a point about Rabelais's "redictes contradictoires" (TL, 10) which is similar to our contention that they constitute a critique of fiction when he distinguishes between "Pantagruélism" and "Rabelaisianism."[20] "Pantagruélism" is an optimistic philosophy regarding the world and human beings, that "good-natured philosophy of joyful living, easy-going companionability and mutual trust,"[21] which is expressed in the Abbaye de Thélème and the "éloge des dettes." The only trouble with it, Keller suggests, is that it is "literature and not life."[22] Life is represented by "Rabelaisianism" and there, cruelty and crudity abound. He says that

---

[20] Abraham Keller, *The Telling of Tales in Rabelais* (Frankfurt: Vittorio Klostermann, 1963), pp. 74-81.
[21] *Ibid.*, p. 77.
[22] *Ibid.*

on a philosophic level, "Rabelaisianism" is a negation of "Pantagruélism." [23]

The only trouble, to re-phrase Mr. Keller, with his antinomy as well as with our own, is that both ideal and "reality," utopia and anti-utopia, are "literature and not life." Gargantua's defeat of Picrochole is "story" as much as Picrochole's fantasy of world conquest; the "Enigme en Prophetie" is every bit as much a literary creation as the Abbaye de Thélème, the dialogues between the "lui" and the "moi" which surround the "eloge des dettes" — both thesis and antithesis exist only as two levels of one fictional world, "the world in Alcofribas' mouth." For the paradox inherent in all these paradoxes is that the critique of fiction which they generate is managed by the fiction itself so that the illusion is always triumphant even as it seems to be broken. It is thus that Alcofribas leads his reader into the labyrinth of fiction's unreal reality and leaves us lost in its mazes. We are confounded, as Rabelais must have been, by literature's duplicity, which reflects the duplicity of language itself — that "...words create the truth and therefore uncreate it since they made it in the beginning; words... at once, in triumph, assert and deny the truth of what they say." [24]

---

[23] *Ibid.*, p. 79.
[24] Colie, p. 95.

CHAPTER III

APOLLO VERSUS BACCHUS:
THE DYNAMICS OF INSPIRATION

Although the prologues to *Gargantua* and to the *Tiers Livre* are very different in tone and in development, their themes are remarkably similar. The subject of both chapters is creative writing. Both begin by comparing the writer to a famous philosopher of antiquity — to Socrates in 1534 and to Diogenes in 1546. Both prologues are concerned with the position of the writer-philosopher in society; how he and his work appear to other men and how the latter will respond to his enterprise. Most significantly, both the prologues to *Gargantua* and to the *Tiers Livre* contain *deffenses et illustrations* of inspiration which describe the source of the writer's genius as a non-rational delirium, a spontaneous welling-up, a state of madness which overcomes him. Words flow from his pen, he says, without conscious premeditation or art. This phenomenon is a source of joy to the writer, but it is also a torture because he cannot control or deny it. At one point in the prologue to the *Tiers Livre*, he speaks rather sadly of being condemned to write: "...telle est ou ma sort ou ma destinée."

We recognize these themes — the writer as inspired, the writer as philosopher, the writer as a *forcené* — as the themes which were developed in the poetry and the treatises of the *Pléiade* poets. However, their "new" attitude toward the creative writer did not assert itself until 1549-1550. Rabelais wrote the prologue to *Gargantua* when Ronsard and DuBellay and their apostles were not quite adolescents; and the prologue to the *Tiers Livre* predates *L'Ode à Michel de l'Hospital*, the first complete literary exposition of inspiration and poetic genius, by at least four years.[1] There are, of course, differences between the idea of inspiration that Rabelais develops in his prologues and the attitude of the *Pléiade* poets. Rabelais was not a poet, he was a prose writer and he was composing in French at a time when serious prose was written in Latin. Moreover, he was unabashedly working within the framework of popular literature, utilizing the whole sweep of "marketplace entertainment."[2] He was not interested, as was *La Brigade,* in the restoration of the high and serious literary genres of the ancients. Nonetheless, with all these differences in mind, the experience of creativity which Rabelais describes in these two prologues is basically similar to the idea of inspiration developed in the poetry of Ronsard, or in the treatise of Pontus de Tyard.[3] The doctrine of genius and creative enthusiasm seems so banal to us now that we forget that it had been lost for a long time. It is possible that the honor of revitalizing that idea, of making inspiration once again a living creative principle, belongs not to the *Pléiade,* but to François Rabelais.

The difficulty in discussing the phenomenon of inspiration as it is described in Rabelais's two prologues is that two opposed conceptions of the writer and his work stand in ironic juxtaposition — the writer as purveyor of high and serious truths, the writer as *amuseur,* a symbolic interpretation versus joyful spontaneity — oil and wine, as Alcofribas puts it, which never blend in a homogenous

---

[1] This poem was not published until 1552: *Les Amours. Ensemble le Cinquiesme des Odes,* but was written in the second half of 1550. See: Henri Chamard, *Histoire de la Pléiade* (Paris: Champion, 1939), I, p. 364. Chamard notes that, although DuBellay had assumed the importance of "cete fureur divine... sans laquele ne fault point que nul espere faire chose qui dure," he had neither defined nor developed the concept of inspiration (*ibid.,* p. 368). Thomas Sebillet, in his *Art Poetique François,* the document which had precipitated *La Deffense,* has been more explicit on this point than DuBellay. See Henri Franchet, *Le Poète et son oeuvre d'après Ronsard* (Paris: Champion, 1922), pp. 6-7. Yet both DuBellay and Sebillet were writing treatises which dealt incompletely and theoretically with divine madness as a *concept,* whereas Ronsard used the idea as a vital creative principle whose dynamics are the subject of his poem.

[2] For the influence of popular literature and traditions on Rabelais, see Mikhail Bakhtin, *Rabelais and His World,* tr. by Helene Iswolsky (Cambridge, Mass.: M. I. T. Press, 1968).

[3] *Solitaire Premier ou Prose des Muses, et de la Fureur Poetique* was published in 1552. It is an exposition, offered in the form of a dialogue between Pontus and his lady, Pasithée, to whom he explains the idea of inspiration.

whole. Yet such an ambivalence has, from the beginning, been intrinsic to the concept of inspiration. It has always been both "many" and "one." Plato, in the *Phaedrus,* had first praised madness in general over the sane mind because it is of divine origin (244d), but he had gone on to delineate not one but *four* divine furors: the prophetic frenzy incited by Apollo, the furor of the mystic overcome by Bacchus, the frenzy inspired by the Muses and the amorous madness incited by Love (244-245c).[4] Now, these four are similar as forms of madness, but each of the gods which govern them has a unique and powerful personality, and the possibilities for conflict between them are endless. But Plato did not comment on their relationship, nor did any of the writers who were influenced by the concept of inspiration.[5] On one hand, poets spoke of madness as a simplex, as DuBellay spoke of *"cete* fureur divine"

---

[4] The two dialogues where Plato discusses inspiration and divine madness most thoroughly are the *Ion* and the *Phaedrus.* Although the most complete exposition is given in the *Phaedrus,* the *Ion* was better known in the Renaissance. Ficino's Latin translation, with his "argument": *Io Platonis, vel de furore poetico,* was published in Venice in 1491. (Franchet, p. 12). Subsequent Latin editions multiplied in Florence, in Venice and in Paris (1518, 1522, 1533). A French translation by Richard Le Blanc was published in 1546, the year of the publication of the *Tiers Livre* (p. 14).

[5] Ficino, it is true, in the Seventh Speech of the *Commentary on the Banquet,* addresses himself to the relationship between the four furors. However, his concern is with divine madness as a philosophic and not as a creative phenomenon. For Ficino, the furors are steps in the hierarchy by which the soul ascends from materiality to unity with God. The following is a paraphrase of his argument:

> The first need is for the poetic madness which calms the discord of the soul by harmony. Next, the mysteries of Bacchus intervene to unify all the parts and direct attention to the mind by which God is worshipped. Now that the soul is made a single out of many, the madness of Apollo is needed to raise the soul above mind, to put it out of time, which is to give it the gift of prophecy. And the final and highest furor is that of Love which unites the soul with God.

See: Marsilio Ficino, *Commentary on the Symposium,* tr. by Sears Jayne (Columbia, Mo.: The University of Missouri Studies, 1944), 19, pp. 230-233.

Pontus de Tyard, in *Le Solitaire Premier,* follows this passage from Ficino very closely. See: *Le Solitaire Premier,* ed. by Silvio Baridon (Geneva: Droz, 1950), pp. 17-18. Despite the subtitle of this work, "Discours des Muses et de la fureur poetique," Pontus discusses divine frenzy less as an esthetic than a philosophic phenomenon: "Car la fureur divine, Pasithée, est l'unique escalier par lequel l'Ame peut trouver le chemin qui la conduise à la source de son souverain bien et felicité derniere." (pp. 16-17.)

(see n. 1). If, on the other, poets such as Ronsard recognized the multiplicity of inspiration, they simply alternated between the furors, combining some, omitting others, as suited their purposes.[6]

François Rabelais recognized the multiplicity of inspiration, but he never required more than two of Plato's four frenzies, since neither the Muses nor Love played a significant role in his imagination. He was left, therefore with the two *frères ennemis* of the Greek Pantheon, Apollo and Bacchus.[7] It is these two gods, as opposed philosophic and art-attitudes, who confront each other in his two prologues. They function in his work much as Nietzsche described in *The Birth of Tragedy*,[8] as poles of the tension which is

---

[6] In *L'Ode à Michel de l'Hospital*, Ronsard emulates Ficino's argument for the *Ion* as he traces the hierarchy by which inspiration descends from God (Jupiter) — to Apollo, to the Muses, to the poet. In this poem, inspiration is perceived as conspicuously "Apollonian"; the poet is a prophet, virtuous and pure. But the picture is quite different in *L'Hymne de Bacchus* where the Muses are rather associated to the god of wine and Apollonian sobriety is vanished:

"Pere, ou me traines-tu? Que veux-tu plus de moy?
Et quoy, n'ay-je pas, Pere, assez chanté de toy?
Evoé je forcene, ah je sens ma poitrine
Chaude des gros bouillons de ta fureur divine."

See: *Oeuvres de Ronsard*, ed. by Isidore Silver (Chicago: University of Chicago Press, 1967), 6, p. 219.

Moreover, Love as well as inspiration is affected by this alternation between the Bacchic and the Apollonian modes in Ronsard's poetry. Terence Cave's work suggests that these concepts may well be used to describe the variance of mood not only from one cycle of love poetry to another, but also *within* each sequence. See: "Ronsard's Bacchic Poetry: from the *Bacchanales* to the *Hymne de l'automne*", *Esprit Créateur*, 10, no. 2 (1970), 104-116; and "Ronsard as Apollo: myth, poetry and experience in a Renaissance sonnet-cycle," *Yale French Studies*, 47 (1972), 76-89.

[7] For a discussion of the Bacchic and poetic furors in *Le Cinquiesme Livre*, see: Masters, *Rabelaisian Dialectic*, pp. 57-67; and Weinberg, *Wine and Will*, 45-92.

[8] Friedrich Nietzsche, *The Birth of Tragedy*, tr. by William A. Haussmann, Vol. 1 of *The Complete Works of Friedrich Nietzsche*, ed. by Oscar Levy (New York: Russell and Russell, 1964). Despite the title and the emphasis of his study, Nietzsche says that comedy as well as tragedy was born of the marriage of Apollo and Dionysus: "And what then...is the meaning of that madness, out of which comic as well as tragic art has grown, the Dionysian madness?" (p. 7).

Nor must we forget that Plato's *Symposium* closes with Socrates' comment (overheard by Aristodemus through a drunken drowsiness) that "the same man might be capable of writing both comedy and tragedy — that

vital to the creative process, as partners of a tempestuous marriage who are continually at odds. Yet "...in like manner as procreation is dependent on the duality of the sexes, involving perpetual conflicts with only periodically intervening reconcilations,"[9] it is from their mating that these prologues and these books are born.

The two opposed art-impulses [10] meet and square off first in the prologue to *Gargantua*. Socrates introduces the conflict between them, for Socrates combines in his nature the Apollonian and the Bacchic principles. He was the disciple of Apollo who took as his own the motto of Apollo's temple at Delphi, "Know thyself." Yet he is described by Alcofribas, paraphrasing the speech of the drunken Alcibiades from Plato's *Symposium*,[11] as ressembling the

---

the tragic poet might be a comedian as well" (223d). Tr. by Michael Joyce in *Plato: The Collected Dialogues including the Letters*, ed. by Edith Hamilton and Huntington Cairns (Princeton, N.J.: Princeton Univ. Press, 1961), p. 574.

[9] Nietzsche, p. 21.

[10] "In order to bring these two tendencies within closer range, let us conceive of them first of all as the separate art-worlds of dreamland and drunkenness..." (*The Birth of Tragedy*, p. 22):

"...Apollo: that measured limitation, that freedom from the wilder emotions, that philosophical calmness of the sculptor-god." (p. 25.) Apollo is "the shaper," the tendency to form and order, and as such is an ethical as well as an esthetic deity: "Apollo, as ethical deity, demands due proportion of his disciples and, that this may be observed, he demands self-knowledge. And thus, parallel to the aesthetic necessity for beauty, there run the demands 'know thyself' and 'not too much,' while presumption and undueness are regarded as the truly hostile demons of the non-Apollonian sphere..." (p. 40).

Bacchus, to the contrary, represents the anarchy of the generative organs as opposed to the ethical sense, the conscience, Apollo: "And now let us imagine to ourselves how the ecstatic tone of the Dionysian festival sounded in ever more luring and bewitching strains into this artifically confined world built on appearance and moderation, how in these strains all the *undueness* of nature, in joy, sorrow and knowledge, even to the transpiercing shriek, became audible: ...The *Undueness* revealed itself as truth, contradiction, the bliss born of pain, declared itself out of the heart of nature." (p. 41.) Bacchus embodies the torture of being obliged to create, he "strives after creation, after the voluptuousness of wilful creation; i.e. constructing and destroying." (p. xxvi.)

[11] In the *Symposium*, Alcibiades also compares Socrates to another follower of Bacchus, Marsyas, the satyr, a comparison which is developed at more length than that of the Silenus. Alcibiades likens the effect of Socrates' speech to the spell cast by Marsyas as he plays the flute, Bacchus' instrument (215b-216a).

"boîtes dites Silènes." Silenus, Alcofribas is careful to point out, "fut...maistre du bon Bacchus." It is by this description of Socrates' double nature that the relationship between Apollo and Bacchus and the conflict between them are established.

In spite of the initial injunction to "Beuveurs tres illustres," the Apollonian principle has the first word. Its *locus* is "inner," it is the spirit of man, of Socrates — the liqueurs inside the Silenus box. In art, Apollo represents the symbolic imagination which hides meaning beneath the "flesh" of words and images, in the marrow within the bone. In this first argument, we are assured that the Bacchic *raillerie* of the book is only a camouflage, and we are urged to penetrate beyond appearances to find its deeper meaning:

> Et, posé le cas qu'*au sens literal* vous trouvez matieres assez joyeuses et bien *correspondentes au nom*, toutesfois pas demourer là ne fault...ains à *plus hault sens interpreter* ce que par adventure cuidiez dict en gayeté de cueur.
> ...puis, par *curieuse leçon et meditation frequente*, rompre l'os et sugcer la sustantificque mouelle — c'est à dire ce que j'entends par *ces symboles Pythagoricques*... car en icelle bien aultre goust trouverez et doctrine plus *absconce*, laquelle vous revelera de tres haultz *sacremens* et *mysteres* horrificques, tant en ce que concerne nostre religion que aussi l'estat politicq et vie oeconomicque. (Italics ours.)

The phrases which have been italicized are very revealing of the mode of Apollonian inspiration. It denigrates the corporeal and the literal, "ce qui correspond au nom," in favor of deep meanings enshrouded in Pythagoric symbols. Its predominant tone in serious; it opposes Bacchic joy. The Apollonian injunction implies gravity of inspiration and intent on the part of the writer and it urges a symmetrical responsibility on the reader — contemplation, meditation and seriousness of interpretation.

Underlying all of Apollo's imperatives is a negative attitude toward language. Words are relegated to the status of mere tools by the symbolic imagination. They are indicators of meaning, but they are not of themselves meaningful. What is meaningful is rather the silence beyond speech; the silence of the writer who could not, or would not, express himself directly, and the silent understanding of his silence on the part of the interpreter. The Apollonian is a curious temptation in the writer — its most perfect expression would ultimately be the blank page.

It is immediately after the talk of "symboles Pythagoricques" and "doctrine plus absconce" quoted above that the Bacchic principle intervenes to contradict the Apollonian injunction almost point by point. It is in this section that inspiration as we commonly think of it is described, a joyful, spontaneous, free-flowing cascade of words. Its symbol is Bacchus' wine. The Bacchic scorns the symbolic, ridicules the allegories that commentators have *calfreté* on the works of writers whom Alcofribas admires, and he warns the reader not to emulate them. We are to take his tale literally. It is empty of high, serious meanings — his are *belles billes vezées* — there is no marrow in them! The attitude which the writer urges on his readers is the joyfulness that Apollo scorned. Moreover, he takes this joy as his own. He refutes the implication that the book is serious and carefully planned and insists that he wrote for fun, spontaneously, not knowing what he would say until it was said, and himself hugely enjoying the surprise.

One begins to understand what Nietzsche meant when he spoke of the Bacchic as the "voluptuousness of wilful creation." (See n. 10.) Creation is described in this second argument as *volupté*. The writer enjoys writing as he enjoys eating and drinking and one activity engenders the other — he writes, he would almost have us believe, *à table*. And his readers are exhorted to drink as they read, to enjoy his story as they would a draught of wine. The bacchanal is described as a banquet,[12] where wine flows to free from constraint the mind and the tongue, and it is in this atmosphere of joy and freedom that words and books are generated. For the Bacchic principle, creation is recreation for the writer and for his audience. It is also re-creation, renewal of the body and the mind of both the giver and receiver of Bacchus' wine.

But to describe the ambiguity of the prologue to *Gargantua* only by outlining the contradictions of its larger structure does not do it justice, since there is ambiguity within each argument. That the Bacchic theme runs all through the prologue has been noted by

---

[12] For a study of banquet imagery and its significance in Rabelais's work, see Bakhtin, *Rabelais and His World*, pp. 278-302.

more than one critic: [13] the beginning address to "Beuveurs tres illustres...," the reference to the speech of the drunken Alcibiades, the comparison of the dog sniffing the bone to a man uncorking a bottle of wine. There is, in general, a tone of Bacchic *raillerie* which runs throughout the Apollonian argument even in its most emphatic moments, undermining it and thus equalizing its force. In the same way, the Bacchic movement of the prologue is mitigated by the influence of Apollo. This is not an illustration of Bacchic enthusiasm, but rather a defense of it. Alcofribas presents a clearly and cogently argued case where the best witnesses: Homer, Plutarch, Heraclitus, *et al.*, are called in. He does not ramble in his arguments, he makes transitions without stumbling. He is, in sum, describing drunkenness with Apollonian art and clarity of mind.

Apollo's oil and Dionysus' wine are, in fact, so mingled as to be profoundly necessary to each other even as they strive to separate. As the two sides of Socrates' nature functioned to maintain the life of the man, so does the sympathetic antipathy between these two art-deities create and sustain the life of Rabelais's books. And thus we must see the ambiguity of the prologue to *Gargantua* as an *affirmation*. This chapter displays the dynamics of the vital tension which exists between Apollo and Bacchus to affirm that the struggle between them is the very condition of the victory of creation as Rabelais describes it in 1534.

The prologue of 1546 is again about creative writing, and again the writer is concerned with how his work will be judged by other men. Once more the writer is equated to a philosopher, here to Diogenes, and his Tub as a container of wine and wisdom is very similar to the Socrates-Silenus-marrowbone images. Above all, the prologue to the *Tiers Livre* also develops these themes and images

---

[13] See: Floyd Gray, "Ambiguity and Point of view in the Prologue to *Gargantua*," *Romanic Review*, 65 (1965), 12-21. Leo Spitzer's thesis might also be mentioned in this context; that Rabelais's neologisms — his use of farcical suffixes (sustanti*fique*) or new root words (*Pantagruélisme*) — undermines his seriousness and reveals his comic, grotesque intent. See: "The Works of Rabelais," in *Literary Masterpieces of the Western World*, ed. by Francis H. Horn (Baltimore: Johns Hopkins, 1953), pp. 126-147; "Rabelais et les 'rabelaisants," *Studi Francesi*, 4 (1960), 401-423; "Le prétendu réalisme de Rabelais," *Modern Philology*, 37 (1939-1940), 139-150; and "Ancora sul prologo al primo libro del *Gargantua* de Rabelais," *Studi Francesi*, 9 (1965), 423-434.

as a dialogue between the Bacchic and the Apollonian art-impulses. This chapter, however, is much less jocular than the prologue to *Gargantua* and much more personal, for it was composed not by the jester Alcofribas Nasier, but by François Rabelais, *medecin*.

Like Socrates, Diogenes is an androgynous creature in whose person the Apollonian and the Bacchic principles coexist. Diogenes is first described as Apollo's disciple. His home is on Cranium, Apollo's *locus*, and he is, in the first paragraph of the prologue, associated with the virtues which result from this superior optic on human affairs — clarity of mind, sight, the sun which is Apollo's emblem. Diogenes' attitude as he looks down on men and judges them, is negative: he is described in this first paragraph as "le philosophe cynic." However, wine is slipped into this encomium of Apollo's virtues by means of a comic lapsus, [14] and in the second paragraph, there follows a praise of Bacchus' nectar. We are urged to: "...en vin non en vain, ainsi plus que physicalement philosopher et desormais estre du conseil Bacchique...." Subsequently, we are assured that this cynic philosopher was also a "philosophe rare et joyeux entre mille."

However, instead of alternating between the Bacchic and the Apollonian points of view as in the prologue of 1534, the prologue to the *Tiers Livre* presents an odd and compelling simultaneity of these contrary impulses. This simultaneity is introduced by the *annominatio* [15] just quoted: the Apollonian *en vain* versus the Bacchic *en vin*, indistinguishable from one another in the homophonous [ã vẽ]. In this ambivalent cry are united all of the various attributes of the two art-impulses which will be developed in the prologue, attributes which are schematized below:

---

[14] "C'est belle chose veoir la clarité du (vin et escuz) Soleil." Jacques Le Clercq interprets the lapsus thus: "Light is beautiful! The sparkle of wine... no, I err; the twinkling of doubloons...no, no, I meant the light of day.... (At last, I make myself clear!). *The Complete Works of Rabelais* (New York: The Modern Library, 1936), p. 293.

[15] For a discussion of this figure of speech as part of the rhetoric of mannerism, see: E. R. Curtius, *European Literature and the Latin Middle Ages*, tr. by Willard R. Trask (New York: Pantheon Books, 1953), pp. 278-280.

	Emblem	*Locus*	Form of Inspiration	Philosophic Attitude	Attitude Toward Speech	Medium of Expression
Apollo: *En Vain*	Oil	Head	Silence, Trance (Angelic)	Skeptic, Serious	Negative	Enigmas, Symbols Silence
Bacchus: *En Vin*	Wine	Generative Organs	Drunkenness, Delirium (Demonic)	Joyful, Optimistic	Positive	Literal *Baragouin*

Throughout two-thirds of the prologue to the *Tiers Livre*, to the point where Diogenes' Tub metamorphoses into a barrel of wine and the [ã vẽ] becomes once and for all, *en vin*, every phenomenon is looked at simultaneously from the Bacchic and the Apollonian points of view. This continual doubling of perspective generates the extreme density of this prologue, one of the most difficult chapters to approach critically in all of Rabelais's work. Because of the problems it poses, this analysis will trace its development step by step.

The first scene of the prologue presents Diogenes *vis-à-vis* the Corinthians as they are fortifying their city against a siege. Here the ambivalent [ã vẽ] is achieved by what we have called in Chapter one the "rhetoric of silence". Diogenes watches the Corinthians "sans mot dire," yet the description of his silence takes up pages and uses hundreds of words, a virtuoso performance unequalled in Rabelais's work. Both Diogenes' silence and Rabelais's *baragouin* are equally meaningful and yet both pronounce, simultaneously, an opposed judgment of the Corinthians as well of Diogenes himself.

The Apollonian *en vain* is pronounced when one regards Diogenes' behavior as symbolic. What is meaningful from this point of view is not the rhetoric, but the silence which lies behind it, and it is the silence of opprobium. Remote from human tempestuousness, high up on Cranium, Diogenes pounds out the judgment that this is a tale full of sound and fury signifying nothing. He is denigrating the Corinthians, all those involved in the active life, all those values which inspire men to action. He is also denigrating himself, the writer, as the word-man. Words cascade forth from his Tub, but they are meaningless noises, silly *baragouin*. His tales, like those of other men, are full of sound and fury and they also signify nothing at all.

But, simultaneously with the *en vain*, the Bacchic *en vin* is pronounced. Here it is the literal which triumphs, the words, the sounds, the noise and confusion which are significant. Taken from this perspective, Diogenes' Tub praises the Corinthians, praises the fun of being alive, hustling and bustling about, laughing and enjoying the task at hand. The *en vin* also praises the writer, for the very reason that Apollo had condemned him — *because* he is the word-man, *because* his creations tickle the eye and the ear and cause laughter, *because* they are meant only to amuse. Further in the prologue the writer will give a defense of Bacchic inspiration, but it is with Diogenes' Tub that inspiration is illustrated. This first scene of the prologue is a "...demonstration as well as a definition of the proposition that literary creation is verbal creation,"[16] a delirium of words which pour forth spontaneously from the writer, as frantically as Diogenes beats his Tub.

Thus, the *en vain* and the *en vin* are pronounced simultaneously, but the reader has the choice of heeding one judgment or the other. This choice depends on two things. It depends, first, as has been said, on whether one takes Diogenes literally or interprets his gestures symbolically. Second, our choice depends on the perspective from which we view Diogenes. For he is both spectator and actor — he is both watching the Corinthians and being watched by them. It is as a spectator of the action that Diogenes' judgment is Apollonian, but as an actor who amuses the Corinthians with his gyrations, he is caught up in Bacchic enthusiasm.

The spectator-actor relationship which exists implicitly between Diogenes and the Corinthians is made explicit in the section of the prologue which follows, when the writer draws the parallel between the philosopher and himself *vis-à-vis* the Parisians. Theatrical imagery dominates this section of the prologue. First of all, the writer

---

[16] Floyd Gray, "Structure and Meaning in the Prologue to the *Tiers Livre*," *L'Esprit Créateur*, 3 (1963), 60.

describes himself an the sidelines as a "spectateur ocieux de tant vaillans, disers et chevalereux personnaiges, qui en veue et spectacle de toute Europe jouent ceste insigne fable et tragicque comedie...," and he compares to "asnes d'Arcadie" those who "par mines en silence signifient qu'ils consentent à la prosopée." Then he himself is put on stage as a jester who amuses as did Diogenes by "remu(ant) mon tonneau Diogenic." Finally, the perspective shifts once more and we find ourselves in the audience looking at the writer "en plein theatre" and judging him as severely as he had first judged the Parisians, as severely as the Egyptians judged the Bactrian camel and the mottled slave mistakenly offered by Ptolemy for their curiosity and amusement.

In this game of shifting perspectives, we designate as Apollonian the function of the spectator, the "looking down at." As a philosophical attitude, the Apollonian is negative, skeptical and ironic. As an aesthetic attitude, it demands "choses belles, eleguantes et perfaictes" — Apollo's form and measure — and the writer is denigrated because he does not conform to it. The Bacchic role is that of the actor, the "tormenter of the Tub," be he Parisian or writer. As a philosophic attitude, it is optimistic and the laughter generated is gay and not ironic. The art that Bacchus produces is uncontrolled, unrestrained — what Apollo terms, "choses ridicules et monstreuses."

By continually juggling these two functions, so that both the Parisians and the writer play the part of both actor and spectator, the lines between them are blurred — both are both spectator and actor at the same time. The result of this game of shifting perspectives is the same inextricable mixture of the Apollonian and the Bacchic injunctions as there was with Diogenes, the same inchoate [ã vẽ].

This middle section of the prologue is of utmost importance, for it is here that the writer explains Bacchic inspiration, which he had illustrated earlier with Diogenes. All the themes that were brought up in the prologue to *Gargantua* are repeated, but here they are developed at greater length and are more specifically allied to the Platonic *furor divinus*. The writer does not work by "art," by a consciously forged technique, but drunkenly, in a delirium when he is overcome by Bacchus. He pretends not to know what he will say until he drinks, but once drunk the words flow from him:

> A ce triballement de tonneau, que feray-je en vostre advis? Par la vierge qui se rebrasse, je ne sçay encores. Attendez un peu que je hume quelque traict de ceste bouteille; c'est mon vray et seul Helicon, c'est ma fontaine caballine, c'est mon unicque enthusiasme. Icy beuvant je delibere, je discours, je resoulz et concluds. Apres l'epilogue je riz, j'escripz, je compose, je boy.

As in the prologue to the *Gargantua*, the writer defends Bacchic inspiration and a spontaneous, natural style by placing himself in a literary tradition. He cites Ennius, Aeschylus, Homer and Cato as writers who, like himself, "beuvoit composant, beuvant composoit." And here, too, he describes creation as *volupté*, using the imagery of the banquet that he had used in the earlier prologue. However, in 1546, he is much more emphatic about the usefulness of recreation. He plays on the double sense of the word *servir* — to be useful and to serve (at table) — and develops the paradox that it is precisely by amusing other men, by serving them "passetemps epicenaires," that he is useful to them. For wine and words and laughter recreate and regenerate men, by liberating them from care and constraint so that they can later take up their tasks with renewed vigor. These paragraphs are a defense of what Bakhtin repeatedly calls "wine's gay and free truth," a truth in which the writer participates and which he makes accessible to other men.

This defense of Bacchic inspiration is immediately undercut as the Apollonian art-impulse surfaces to denigrate the usefulness of Bacchic amusement. Bacchus' art displeases Apollo because it has no form, no beauty, and offends by its grotesque excessiveness. And so, exhausted by the long struggle in him between these two voices, the writer ends this second movement of the prologue by throwing himself on the mercy of his readers and hoping that there will be among them a few *Pantagruélistes* who will enjoy his story and take it in the spirit it was offered.

This note of rather wistful hopefulness is only momentary, however, for Diogenes' Tub metamorphoses into a barrel of wine and Bacchus' victory over Apollo is achieved. The [ã vɛ̃] becomes, once and for all, *en vin!* The call to drink from Diogenes' cask affirms the endeavors of the Corinthians and the Parisians at the same time as it praises the writer himself, the source of his inspiration and the grotesque images which surge from it. For wine is a symbol of the primal energy in all its forms, be it inspiration or action. It is the blind force in all men which makes them live and act and create despite the councils of reason which tell them that their endeavors are in vain. Though wine has been diluted in this prologue, the oil and water have been removed from it. We approach the bottom of the barrel now, and we are promised that more joy and more words await us there:

> Ainsi demeurera le tonneau inexpuisible. Il a source vive et vene perpetuelle.... C'est un vray Cornucopie de joyeuseté et raillerie.... Bon espoir y gist au fond, comme en la bouteille de Pandora; non desespoir, comme on bussart des Danaïdes.

However, it is not joy that is found in the deepest part of the barrel; to the contrary, it is a place filled with horror. Nietzsche warns that the Bacchic "voluptuousness of wilful creation" involves both "constructing and destroying" (See n. 8). In the last paragraphs of the Prologue, we participate in the destruction, in the dark rites of the bacchanal which always follow the revelry by a dreadful logic. For the barrel metamorphoses again, into a cudgel, "le baston de Diogenes," and the prologue ends with the writer's hysteria as he uses the stick to beat and to "kill" his enemies.

And the writer himself is under attack, even as he attacks his enemies. These last paragraphs are also an illustration of Bacchic enthusiasm, but here inspiration is perceived as an agony rather than a joy, a death — the torture of the writer by Bacchus who attacks his mortal frame and "tears him from himself."[17] This development had occurred as well, in a more abbreviated form, at the end of the prologue to *Gargantua,* and in both prologues, the final flaying and dismemberment had been prefigured by the domi-

---

[17] Edgar Wind discusses the theme of the torture of the mortal by the god who inspires him to explain the iconography of Raphael's "Flaying of Marsyas." See: *Pagan Mysteries in the Renaissance* (Harmondsworth, Eng.: Penguin Books, 1967), pp. 171-176. Note, too, the similarity with Ronsard's *Hymne de Bacchus* where the poet is also attacked by the god of wine. (See n. 6.)

nant images: the breaking-open of the Silenus box, the chewing of the marrowbone, the beating of the Tub, the tapping of the keg of wine. For it is as Alcibiades suggested in the *Symposium*, the "container" must be broken in order to obtain the precious liqueur within it. Creation is contingent upon destruction — it is born from the "death" of reason. In order to obtain truth and clarity of mind, the writer must submit to such a Dionysian ordeal. He must descend into the darkness in order to find light.[18]

It is thus that the struggle between the Bacchic and the Apollonian art-impulses in the prologues to *Gargantua* and the *Tiers Livre* ends with the necessary and terrible triumph of the Bacchic. The geometry of the two prologues might be traced as a vacillating line which is imperceptibly but implacably pulled downward, from the top of Apollo's mountain to the depths of Bacchus' barrel and still deeper, into the dark earth. This downward movement will also predominate in the quest of the *Tiers Livre* and it leads from there into the nether world of the *Quart Livre*. As he talks about creativity and as he creates, Rabelais traces the same path downward into hell that great visionary poets have always traced, those who dared recognize the vortex in themselves and in the world. Orpheus, Dante, Baudelaire, Poe, Rimbaud — these are his true brothers.

---

[18] Nietzsche discusses the paradox of creation contingent upon destruction thus:

> Indeed, it seems as if the myth sought to whisper in our ears that wisdom, especially Dionysian wisdom, is an unnatural abomination, and that whoever, through his knowledge, plunges nature into an abyss of annihilation, must also experience the dissolution of nature in himself. (*The Birth of Tragedy*, p. 75.)

CHAPTER IV

THE BIRTH OF THE *TIERS LIVRE*

In the *Pantagruel*, Thaumaste conducts his *tour des sages* in search of that inconceivable abstraction, "la vérité seule" (P, 18-20). No indication is given of the specific nature of the questions which trouble him, and it is from this lack of specificity that much of the comic of this episode derives. The man who conducts such a quest is by nature an abstraction, a contrivance — one which lends itself as well to the comic writer as to the serious philosopher. For in life, one searches for truth in relation to some concrete issue, not as truth *qua* truth. Thaumaste's concerns detach him from life-as-it-is, and it is precisely in the name of the crudest aspects of life-as-it-is that he is ridiculed.

However, Panurge's quest in the *Tiers Livre* is less easy to ridicule because he is seeking resolution of a very specific and concrete dilemma — which is a measure of how the problems of truth and knowledge had come to preoccupy Rabelais in the fourteen years which separate the *Pantagruel* from the *Tiers Livre*. Marriage is used by him as the paradigm and the focus for all the uncertainties and paradoxes of human life, uncertainties which make the quest for truth natural and imperative, for no other human situation involves the individual as totally as marriage and so thoroughly determines the climate of one's whole life. Panurge's quest for a resolution of this problem is a quest that most of us have undertaken.

Of all the perplexities of marriage, the most crucial ones center on the troublesome relationship with the existential "other"; she who shares the ambiguity of the individual and compounds it to infinity with her own ambiguity.[1] Marriage is terrifying because in no other human situation is one so totally at the mercy of the set of contingencies and contradictions which the "other" embodies. It is this problem which conditions the debates on the nature of women in the *Tiers Livre*, an issue which transcends the narrow context of the *querelle des femmes*. For the eternally mysterious Feminine has always been the most appropriate symbol of the "other" and union with Her has always set up the cycle of attraction and repulsion that Panurge manifests. He anatomizes this dilemma with clarity in chapter nine as he ricochets back and forth between the *pro* and *contra* of marriage, imagining the possibilities for good and for evil that are present in their plenitude in Her. It is the problem of the "other" which prevents him from marrying, at the same time as it pushes him forward to find the truth, the Word, which will define and determine his relationship to Her.

Nonetheless, had Rabelais only intended to use marriage as a metaphor of an existential dilemma, he might have chosen another human situation. What makes marriage so absolutely appropriate is that it is also a metaphor for creativity and, as such, it transposes and continues into the body of the *Tiers Livre*, the writer's debate with himself in the Prologue as to the value of creative writing. The author, too, is troubled by the problem of the "other," and he faces the unknown reader with the same trepidation as Panurge faces the yet-unfound wife — both vacillate "entre craincte et espoir" (P). It is no mistake that Panurge is introduced as the governor of Salmigondin, the province that Alcofribas was awarded in the *Pantagruel* (32), for the hopes and fears of the writer and his character are identical. Both are primarily concerned with "paternity" — with children "of the mind" as well as of the body. Both Panurge and the writer may be described as Panurge describes himself, as "faiteur(s) et createur(s)" (TL, 3) who emulate the divine in creating something from nothing, from their own living substance, "pierres vives" (6) which are children and books. It is this enterprise which is debated by the entire *Tiers Livre*, Prologue as well as consultations — the *pro* and *contra* of creation and creativity of all sorts, intellectual and artistic as well as physical.

---

[1] See the discussion of the woman as "other" in Simone de Beauvoir, *Le Deuxième Sexe* (Paris: Gallimard, 1949), esp. the Introduction, pp. 11-35.

These thematic links between the Prologue and the body of the *Tiers Livre* are the basis for what will be the underlying assumption of this chapter — that the quest undertaken in this book has both artistic and philosophic values which are inextricably welded together. It is the metaphor of marriage which consolidates their union, for marriage is used by Rabelais to focus on problems which are both existential and creative, and both dimensions of the dilemma are present at every juncture of the *Tiers Livre*. Panurge's wondering as to whether or not he should marry must be seen as a transposition and a continuation of the writer's dialogue with himself in the Prologue on the joys and the dangers, the value of creative writing. The writer thus shares in the quest that his characters undertake, for the truth sought in the *Tiers Livre* is one which will solve both the philosophic and the artistic problems which the book raises. It is a quest for the *Logos* itself, the Word which is perfect truth and perfect expression of that truth.

Marriage, in the usual sense, remains only a subject of conversation in the *Tiers Livre*, for no woman is found and no marriage is consummated. However, there is in Nietzsche's sense, a very vigorous and tempestuous marriage; one which "gives birth" to the book and sustains its life. Panurge and Pantagruel each take up one of the voices heard in the dialogue of the Prologue, the dialogue between Bacchus and Apollo, and it is by their friendship that the sympathetic antipathy between these two gods provides the basic dynamism of the book as of its introduction. United by deep love, these two friends are unalterably opposed in their attitude toward the quest and in the direction they would take it. The life of the *Tiers Livre* springs from their successive "peaceful battles": "... both these two so heterogenous tendencies run parallel to one another, for the most part openly at variance and continually inciting one another to new and more powerful births..." [2]

The relationship between Panurge and Pantagruel is a multidimensional one; they incorporate psychological, philosophical and artistic values. As the "echo" technique of chapter nine makes

---

[2] Nietzsche, *Birth of Tragedy*, p. 21. Again, Nietzsche's premises are taken for granted in this chapter, as well as his characterization of Apollo and Bacchus. See Chapter III, n. 10.

clear — where Pantagruel's answers are only re-statements of Panurge's questions — they function both internally and externally to one another. As voices in an internal dialogue, they display the terms of the psychological ambivalence which operated in the Prologue. This inner doubleness is compounded by the perceptual duplicities of the world and by the two epistemological stances that can be taken in face of this doubleness — the two divergent attitudes toward life and toward experience that Apollo and Bacchus represent. And, paralleling their psychological and philosophical value, Panurge and Pantagruel confront one another as opposed art-impulses: as Form versus Creative Energy and as the two conflicting kinds of inspiration that Bacchus and Apollo represent.

It is as divergent philosophic attitudes that Panurge and Pantagruel first confront one another, in the chapters which precede the consultations (1-9). These chapters contain the famous "éloge des dettes" (2-4), and it is the function of this episode to establish the dialectical form of the *Tiers Livre* as well as to delineate the major points of view which will confront one another as the consultations proceed. As they debate the wisdom of borrowing and lending, Panurge and Pantagruel present the case of Physis versus that of *Nomos*, the ethical-moral sense. Panurge's concern is always with nature, it is his constant frame of reference. His argumentation in the "éloge des dettes" is, to be sure, a comic justification of his vice, but insofar as he deduces from borrowing and lending an entire cosmology, he is serious. He pictures the natural world as a great chain of being, in which all the parts contribute to one another to sustain universal life; and it is by placing himself in this chain that he justifies his function first as a creator of debts and then of children. When Pantagruel paid his debts, he cut the cord which bound Panurge to nature and this separation is intolerable to him, for it is union with nature that he is compelled to seek and to celebrate. He sees in the union of marriage a means of ending his separation. It represents to him an "exchange" which does not involve money and which will work to perpetuate universal life and universal harmony.

Pantagruel, to the contrary, is the urge toward separation from nature and from other men. He is what Nietzsche termed the *prin-*

ciple of individuation.[3] It is in the name of individuation that he rebuts Panurge's arguments in favor of borrowing and lending (5). He eulogizes instead the self-contained man who stands apart from others and who borrows and lends only when his own best efforts have been exhausted. And he cannot convince Panurge of the justice of his philosophy any more than Panurge can persuade him. The "éloge des dettes" hence comes to a close with Pantagruel's exercise of the kingly prerogative of ordering his subject to be silent and to obey.

As the Apollonian principle of individuation, Pantagruel manifests and advocates the clarity of mind which results from his detachment. He continually reproaches Panurge for not knowing his mind, not being assured of his will (10), being blinded by self-love (32). In contrast to Panurge, whose frame of reference is always nature and the natural world, Pantagruel's examples are usually bookish, intellectual, and they argue for "law and order" versus the anarchy of nature. As *Nomos*, the Governor incarnate, any excessiveness, be it spending the revenue of Salmigondin in fourteen days or appearing in a toga without underwear (7), is anathema to him. One must, according to Pantagruel, conserve one's goods and one's energies (2) and, regardless of private opinions and desires, always follow "le commun usaige" (7). And, though he feels that we owe others mutual love and affection (5), Pantagruel loves from a distance. His concern is that one be in harmony with his surroundings, calm and detached from human imbroglio and tempestuousness:

> Jamais ne se tourmentoit, jamais ne se scandalizoit. Aussi eust il esté bien forissu du deificque manoir de raison, si aultrement se feust contristé ou altéré. Car tous les biens que le ciel couvre et que la terre contient en toutes ses dimensions: haulteur, profondité, longitude, et latitude, ne sont dignes d'esmouvoir nos affections et troubler nos sens et espritz (2).

Panurge, to the contrary, "tousjours se tourmentoit, tousjours se scandalizoit." All human things move his affections and engage his senses. He is *engagement* incarnate. Whereas Pantagruel is Rabelais's

---

[3] *Ibid.*, p. 25.

M. Teste, Panurge's *locus* is the generative organs which, significantly, are freed in the *Tiers Livre* of all constraint. He is the creative principle, the Bacchic fool, blind and unreflective. As such, he is as vulnerable to circumstances as Pantagruel is invulnerable to them, for Panurge is by his nature dependent on others to fulfill his functions. He is thus moved this way and that by events, in contrast to Pantagruel whose bemused equanimity is the fixed point of the *Tiers Livre.*

As the consultations begin, and as they proceed, the artistic implications of the friendship between Panurge and Pantagruel emerge and are melded to the epistemological attitudes they embody. First, they stand as the Bacchic creative energy versus the Apollonian demand for form and order. It is Panurge who generates the quest and it is he who sustains it. He persists in his creative folly throughout the *Tiers Livre,* pushing blindly onward, despite the councils of reason which tell him that his enterprise is in vain. It is his blind striving after creation — creation as an instinct — which moves the book forward. However, if Panurge generates the *Tiers Livre,* it is Pantagruel who builds it. It is Pantagruel who leads Panurge one after another to all the oracles, Pantagruel who sets up the Symposium with Hippothadée, Rondibilis and Trouillogan. It is Pantagruel who suggests to Panurge that he consult the fools Bridoye and Triboulet. Pantagruel lends to Panurge the Apollonian "art of the shaper"[4] without which this creative energy could not realize itself. Thus, artistically as well as philosophically, the *Tiers Livre* is born of the equipoise between the Bacchic and the Apollonian principles — nature's centrifugal and centripetal forces whose tension sustains art as well as life.

Paralleling their *concordia discors* as Form versus Energy, Pantagruel and Panurge also relate to one another as Bacchic versus Apollonian inspiration. The body of the *Tiers Livre* is herein the reverse of the Prologue, for there Bacchic inspiration was abundantly defended and illustrated. The Apollonian principle functioned primarily as the counter-weight, the negative attitude toward it. In the consultations, because prevoyance is the issue, it is rather Apollonian inspiration which is displayed over and over again and here the Bacchic functions as the counterpoint. To discuss the

---

[4] *Ibid.,* p. 21.

relationship between them, we turn to the two consultations which best explore the nature of Apollonian inspiration and the Bacchic reaction to it, two consultations which are very similar to one another; the dream episode (13-14), and the consultation with the dying poet, Raminagrobis (21).

When Pantagruel suggests to Panurge in Chapter thirteen that he sleep and dream himself the truth of whether or not he should marry, he is asserting a belief common to the Neo-platonists, that the irrational, "appetitive" functions of man, as Ficino called them, are superior to the intellect as a mode of cognition.[5] This belief had as its origin and justification Plato's theory of Recollection, which holds that each man carries within himself the memory of the Ideas, a memory lost and obscured when the soul was implanted in the body. (*Phaedo* 73-76.) The soul is freed to return to its heavenly home, to "remember," only in privileged beings at privileged moments when they temporarily surmount the pull downward of the body. (*Phaedrus* 246-250.) Pantagruel uses the metaphor of the nurse slipping away from the sleeping child to describe the separation of the soul from the body, and his exposition of the theory of Recollection is one of his most lyrical moments in the *Tiers Livre*:

> De là receoit participation insigne de sa prime et divine origine, et en contemplation de ceste infinie et intellectuale sphaere, le centre de laquelle est en chascun lieu de l'univers, la circunference poinct (c'est Dieu scelon la doctrine de Hermes Trismegistus) à laquelle rien ne advient, rien ne passe, rien ne dechet, tous temps sont praesens, note non seulement les choses passées en mouvemens inferieurs, mais aussi les futures, et, les raportant à son corps et par les sens et organes d'icelluy les exposant aux amis, est dict vaticinatrice et prophete (13).[6]

---

[5] For a complete discussion of Ficino's theory of natural appetites and their superiority as a cognitive mode, see: Kristeller, *The Philosophy of Marsilio Ficino*, pp. 171-288.

[6] For the history of the image of the sphere and the circle, see: Abel Lefranc, "Marguerite de Navarre et le Platonisme de la Renaissance," in *Grands écrivains français de la Renaissance*, pp. 175-185. Lefranc says that it was Rabelais who gave this admirable comparison "droit de cité" in French literature — Mlle. de Gournay borrowed it from him and in turn transmitted it to Pascal (p. 172). As to the source for Rabelais himself, Lefranc is of the opinion that, although this metaphor (traceable to the

The idea of inspiration was, in Plato, cognate to the theory of Recollection, for as Socrates explained in the *Phaedrus*, the four kinds of divine madness are the means by which the poet, the prophet, the mystic and the lover regain their wings and "recall" the divine truths they have forgotten. (244-245a, 248.) However, the four kinds of madness, of inspiration, were quite different, although their goal, knowledge, was the same. What Pantagruel is describing here is only one of these four frenzies, the one to which the word "frenzy" scarcely seems to apply, the prophetic madness whose medium is dream and trance.

Apollo's way is the harshest and straitest gate of all, in its very essence life-denying, and Pantagruel makes this clear as he goes on to stipulate to Panurge the conditions he must fulfill in order to have a prophetic dream. The most divine part of him, "(c'est *Noũs* et Mens)", must be tranquil and peaceful; and so that this quietude may be accomplished, Panurge must detach himself from "toute affection humaine: d'amour, de haine, d'espoir et de craincte" (13). The body must be brought into obeyance, its cries silenced. Although Pantagruel affirms the union of the body and the soul and states that he opposes fasting, the diet he prescribes for Panurge is that of an ascetic, a bit of fruit and water to drink — hardly a meal suited to the lusty, wine-drinking Panurge.

Sleep is a temporary death, and Apollonian inspiration as Pantagruel describes it is contingent upon "killing" the body, upon "dying". It is thus that the dream episode is linked thematically with the consultation with the poet, Raminagrobis, who is in actuality, dying (21). He is inspired by a god to compose poetry, but his verse is the gift of Apollo and not of the Muse of poetry. He literally fulfills Apollo's requirement of detachment from the body and from earthly life — he is already half-way into the other world and he hears the angels speaking to him of future things more clearly than he hears Panurge and Epistemon. These intimations of immortality, offered him by Apollo, are recorded in the poet's "swan song."

---

pseudo-Hermes) was "dans l'air" at the time, Rabelais probably read it in the works of the two philosophers where the formula is complete: Cusanus' *De ludo globi* I. ii; and Ficino's *Theologia Platonica* L. XVIII. (*Ibid.*, pp. 177-181.)

The funereal overtones of Apollonian inspiration are already clear to Panurge in Chapter fifteen when he expresses his distaste for the conditions under which his dream took place. As the Bacchic principle, Panurge attacks the very premises of this method of divination. Characteristically, he holds up as an example and as a justification for himself, the natural world, the world that Apollo denies and would kill. His stringent asceticism is called by Panurge a "scandale en nature":

> "Nature a faict le jour pour soy exercer, ... La nuyct vient; il convient cesser du labeur et soy restaurer par bon pain, bon vin, bonnes viandes; puys quelque peu esbaudir, coucher et reposer pour au lendemain, estre frays et alaigres au labeur comme davant (15).

It is important that Panurge here opposes Pantagruel by using the imagery of the banquet and that he stresses the regenerative value of wine. For Bacchus opposes the banquet to Apollo's funeral. Wine frees the mind from constraint as sleep does, but rather than denying the body, wine uses it as an instrument. As Diogenes in the Prologue beat his tub until he reached a state of hysteria, so Bacchus heightens the pleasures of the body to turgidity, to a state of madness when the god himself can speak. Words pour forth as his wine is spilled, and words and wine affirm life with the creation of works of art and with the re-creation of men. Wine has the color of blood and the odor of life and it is by praising wine that Panurge rejects the sacramental oil with which the Apollonian Pantagruel has anointed him.

All of their values as opposed philosophies of life and as art-attitudes are brought to bear and focussed as Panurge and Pantagruel confront one another as the two primal interpreters of the enigma of human destiny. The *Tiers Livre* combines the *procédé Thaumaste* with the format of the "Enigme en Prophétie" in such a way that "interpretation," that literary problem, becomes the very condition of the philosophic quest. It is no mistake that the first oracle which Panurge and Pantagruel consult together is a book, the Virgilian and Homeric lots (10-12), for the world of the *Tiers Livre* is constituted as a text on whose successive pages are written hieroglyphs and enigmas.[7] All of the oracular consultants express themselves as obliquely as Panurge's dream and Raminagrobis' poem, and thus the Book of the World cannot just be *read*, it must be *interpreted*. Panurge and Pantagruel face these enigmas as did Gargantua and Frère Jean — as literary critics or as poets according to Baudelaire. The task which is set the quester after truth is to traverse a "forêt de symboles" and glose the text of the world. Truth is described as having its *locus* beneath what is apparent to us and the "sustantificque mouelle" must be torn from its deceptive covering.

Rabelais got the image of the "cipher-writing of nature" from the Neo-platonists,[8] but contrary to them, he posits the interpretation of the ciphers as a problem. They had assumed that an initiate into the mysteries would always be able to understand the truth behind the symbols. Rabelais, to the contrary, plays on the subjectivity that the word "interpretation" implies. The image of the enigma is used by him in the body of the *Tiers Livre* for the same purpose as he used theatrical imagery in the prologue — as a foil against which a game of shifting perspectives is played out. This game is a serious one, for it questions the very premises of the quest. The *Tiers Livre* certainly does not deny a transcendant truth. To the contrary, it is consistently affirmative about the existence of the Divine. However, the *Tiers Livre* does seriously question whether man, confined to the sensible and to the relative, and to a language expressive of these dimensions, can ever attain knowledge of timeless universals. From our point of view, "truth" is always only "interpretation". And human affairs, if we are honest about it, are like the silenus box — for every truth, the opposite may also be true. Which "truth" we choose over another depends on optic, on perspective, on error, and by continually juggling perspectives, this lesson is reiterated over and over again.

The dream episode is of outstanding importance to the *Tiers Livre*, for of all the oracles, it is the only one to comment specifically on the problem of interpretation. What is more important, it describes the relationship between inspiration and interpretation as a problematic one. Panurge is, in this episode, in the unique position

---

[7] For a discussion of the Book as Symbol, see E. R. Curtius, *European Literature and the Latin Middle Ages*, pp. 302-347.
[8] See our Introduction, pp. 28-30; and Chapter I, pp. 43-44.

of being both the inspired oracle and one of the interpreters. As the oracle, he expresses himself as all the other prophets do, in oblique symbols. However, his interpretation is not, as would be expected, privileged — to the contrary. For prophecy and interpretation are delineated by Pantagruel as deriving from two different *loci* in man. The one is a function of madness, it is divinely inspired and offers glimpses of high truths. It is therefore constrained to speak in: "... amphibologies, equivocques et obscuritez..." (19), for the nature of its visions transcends the capacity of straightforward human speech. The prophet thus requires an interpreter; and interpretation, conversely, is an acquired skill requiring reason and art:

> Vray est qu'elle (l'âme) ne les (ses visions) raporte en telle syncerité comme les avoit veues, obstant l'imperfection et fragilité des sens corporelz...
> Pourtant reste à ces vaticinations somniales interprete qui soit dextre, saige, industrieux, expert rational et absolu onirocrites et oniropole... (13).

It is thus that Panurge finds himself, in this episode, praised as an oracle and disqualified as an interpreter. He conspicuously lacks the rational expertise, the objectivity, to interpret correctly the shapes which surge from his own madness.

Panurge's disqualification, however, does not automatically assure the superiority of Pantagruel's interpretation. For his credentials are also cast into doubt by the dream episode. His interpretations, too, are seen to stem from a bias rather than from superior objectivity and insight, and Frère Jean hints that this is so when he teases Pantagruel about his exposition of the gates of ivory versus the gates of "horn":

> Vous voulez inferer (dist frere Jan) que les songes des coquz cornuz, comme sera Panurge, Dieu aydant et sa femme, sont tousjours vrays et infallibles (13).

Exactly so. All of the oracles are "neuter," they are vessels into which any number of interpretations may be poured and fit neatly. That Pantagruel invariably chooses to interpret them to Panurge's detriment is a function of his bias as the Apollonian interpreter. He is as condemned to his nay-saying as Panurge is to his Bacchic yea-saying.

Critics have always argued over whether it is Panurge or Pantagruel who is the "correct" interpreter, the *porte-parole* of the author, but to choose one of them over the other is to destroy much of their significance and much of the meaning of the *Tiers Livre*. It is more to the point to remark that neither is objective, that both reflect a bias, for this deeply affects the central problem of the *Tiers Livre*, the problem of truth. And paradoxically, it affects the problem of truth in two opposed ways. In one sense, the equipoise of the contradictory interpretations of Panurge and Pantagruel conveys a skepticism that the object of the quest can ever be attained. Truth seems doomed to remain wrapped in enigma since each man is condemned to interpret life's symbols to accord with his own needs, his desires, his prejudices. The only objective truth that can be derived from the interpretation paradoxes of the *Tiers Livre* is that man is trapped in a "relativisme angoissant". [9]

However, at the same time as the consultations deride the quest for truth, the praise it and push it forward. The balancing of thesis and antithesis, with no possible synthesis, leaves each consulation open-ended and thus each one generates the movement toward the other. The ability of both protagonists to refute the other's arguments creates doubt in both of them as to the validity of their interpretation, and so they both push eagerly forward in hope of finding an unequivocal answer to settle the dispute once and for all. The need for the Answer becomes ever stronger in Panurge, and Pantagruel, despite his conviction that the quest is in vain becomes as deeply involved in it as Panurge. He, too, is caught up in the desire to go "beyond interpretation" to the *Logos*, that point in infinity where the parallel lines of paradox intersect.

As important as these considerations are, the problematic relationship between inspiration and interpretation as it is explored in the dream episode raises a consideration which is even more fundamental to the *Tiers Livre* — the problem of the relative superiority of intuition and reason as modes of cognition. This problem conditions the conflict between Panurge and Pantagruel and it deeply affects the problem of truth which the quest raises. For before knowledge can be pursued, it must be decided which path will lead to truth. Intuition is praised by Pantagruel over reason in the dream

---

[9] Spitzer, "Le prétendu réalisme," p. 145.

episode as the means by which man may glimpse eternal verities, and although it is not explicitly stated elsewhere, this is the assumption which underlies all of the oracular consultants. While this assumption is not directly attacked in the dream episode, it is shown to be, at best theoretical, at worst doubtful. For as folly is constrained to speak in enigmas, it is contingent upon reason as an interpreter, and as the consultations reiterate over and over again, more than one interpretation can be offered and logically substantiated. Folly's contingency on reason negates its efficacy as a mode of knowledge and all of the oracles falter and fail on this point. Not one of the oracles in this first cycle of consultations, from the *sors virgilianes* through Her Trippa,[10] resolves Panurge's problem one whit, and the quest, initiated to go "beyond interpretation," finds itself with the oracles bogged down and defeated by the very problem which generated it. Her Trippa marks this defeat. He stands as the *reductio ad absurdum* of the premises which underlie all of these supernatural sources of wisdom.

Since folly has failed, the *Tiers Livre* turns, with the second cycle of consultants — Hippothadée, Rondibilis and Trouillogan — to reason. Accordingly, the structure and orientation of the consultations undergo a change. The formula of the enigma disappears and the dialogue between Panurge and Pantagruel is set aside. Panurge poses to each of these representatives of the "earthly estates" two questions: "Dois-je me marier?" and "Serai-je cocu si je me marie?", and each of the three addresses himself to these questions calmly and coherently, with all the authority of the scriptures, of medicine and of philosophy behind him. However, the rub is that they answer both questions in the affirmative: Yes, Panurge should marry if he wants to and if he needs to; and yes, regrettably, the chances are that he will be betrayed and mistreated by his wife. Two yesses, to Panurge, quite understandably do not resolve his problem.

---

[10] The consultation with Frère Jean (26-28) follows Her Trippa and precedes the Symposium, but it does not belong to either cycle. It must rather be seen as the transition between the two groups of consultations, for it contains elements of both. Frère Jean's down-to-earth approach to Panurge's problem places him among the "earthly estates" who follow. Yet, as the bells are *interpreted* by Panurge, this consultation is also a throwback to the formula of the oracles. The consultation with Frère Jean might be called "l'oracle des cloches de Varennes."

With the "earthly estates," the philosophic and literary values inherent in the problem of interpretation temporarily diverge, for this cycle of consultants addresses itself solely to the moral-ethical problem of judgment. As Hippothadée, Rondibilis and Trouillogan confront the perplexities afforded by Panurge's problem, they prove themselves to be good judges, but the paradox is that they are good judges because they do not judge. As men of reason and conscience, they are constrained to give equal weight to all the arguments *pro* and *contra* marriage and thus they can do no more than re-state the problem. In this, they ressemble the judges of the case cited by Dolabella which is used by Pantagruel in chapter forty-four as the paradigm of the "perplexitez du jugement humain". These judges refrained from pronouncing judgment on the woman of Smyrna, for although she was clearly guilty of killing her second husband and her son by him, she was justified in her crime by their murder of her child by a first marriage. Both her case and Panurge's so confound the categories of judgment: innocence-guilt, *pro-contra*, right-wrong, that a "good" judge, a man of reason and conscience, must refrain from arbitrarily tipping the scales in either direction.

However, their abstention obviously makes them bad judges, too, and it is the function of Trouillogan to point out their failure (35-36). His monosyllabic replies to Panurge's questions: "Ni l'un ni l'autre et tous les deux," are a *reductio ad absurdum* of the kind and witty rhetoric of Hippothadée and Rondibilis. Trouillogan demonstrates reason's inability to deal with complex human problems. For reason is logically constrained to approve and disapprove of both prongs of a logical cleftstick and hence parodies its own processes as it points out its own limitations. Pantagruel and Gargantua, who was resurrected from the dead to attend this particular consultation, had both initially approved of his paradoxes as a sign of superior wisdom (35). But as the consultation proceeds, they reject and attack him — Gargantua is particularly angry (36). For reason unaccompanied by folly degenerates into Trouillogan's brand of pithy skepticism. His mumbo-jumbo is as meaningless as Her Trippa's hocus-pocus, and Panurge's despair after he leaves Trouillogan is boundless. The truth he is seeking and has sought for so long still remains, unattainable, at the bottom of a bottomless well (36). Both reason and folly have been explored as ways to knowledge and both have failed. There appears to be no other road that the quest for truth may take.

However, the wise Pantagruel has yet another suggestion — that Panurge "prendre conseil de quelque fol" (37) — and with it, despair is banished and the *Tiers Livre* is renewed. This chapter is the equivalent of that point in the Prologue where Diogenes' Tub turns into a barrel filled with wine's gay and free truth. This new joy and freedom is signalled by the carnival imagery which dominates in this chapter. The "official world" is turned topsy-turvy and the bottom of its hierarchy becomes the apex of the carnavalesque world. Here the fool is king, the wise man plays the clown and, most important, the fool Seigny Joan is lauded as the wisest judge.

The praise of the "Fool as Judge" on which chapter thirty-seven centers represents a new departure for the *Tiers Livre* because it re-shuffles the categories of the book and redefines the relation of madness and reason to one another. With the oracular consultants, it had been the function of folly to compose enigmas; the task of interpretation had been specifically assigned by Pantagruel to reason (13). But the earthly estates have demonstrated that reason, far from interpreting human affairs, further complicates them by confronting one with enigmas just as insoluble as those offered by folly. So Pantagruel puts the quest back into the hands of fools where it began, but now they, and not reasonable men, will act as *interpreters*. Madness, he suggests, may well be superior to reason as the judge and arbiter of the perplexities of Panurge's dilemma. [11]

In order to "transvalue" folly into wisdom, [12] wisdom must first be ridiculed as folly, and accordingly Bridoye begins by satirizing the *Judges as Fools*. His insistence in the courtroom that he judges

---

[11] Puys que, par les responses des saiges n'estes à plein satisfaict, conseillez vous à quelque fol...

Vous acquiescerez en ceste raison: car comme celluy ...qui ne pert occasion quelconque de acquerir et amasser biens et richesses...vous appellez saige mondain, quoy que fat soit il en l'estimation des Intelligences coelestes; ainsi faut il, pour davant icelles saige estre, je dis sage et praesage par aspiration divine et apte à recepvoir benefice de divination, se oublier soymesmes, issir hors de soymesmes, vuider ses sens de toute terrienne affection, purger son esprit de toute humaine sollicitude et mettre tout en non chaloir. Ce que vulgairement est imputé à follie." (37)

[12] It is Edgar Wind who speaks of the "transvaluation of values" accomplished by the Neo-platonists. (*Pagan Mysteries*, pp. 53-62, 68-71.)

"comme vous aultres" (39-42) is, in the strictest sense, a satire of law and the courts. In the largest sense, it is a criticism of all traditional and rational criteria of judgment, the criteria used by Hippothadée, Rondibilis and Trouillogan. All men, all judges call in textbooks and test cases, they weigh the sacks *pro* and *contra*, but if they judge at all, they must judge as Bridoye judges, according to a mental casting of the dice, or else resign themselves to perpetual suspension of judgment. For in most cases, no choice can reasonably be made, and if one is made, it is of necessity arbitrary and subjective. All the paraphernalia of the law is ridiculed by Bridoye as a smokescreen behind which the foolish judges hide their failure from themselves and from others.

The second theme of this episode, the praise of the *Fool as Judge*, also centers on the metaphor of "casting the dice," but Bridoye's wise folly differs from that of the foolish wise men, for he casts the dice for other reasons and to other ends. Bridoye, unlike those who are judging him, sees the perplexities of human judgment and he recognizes his inability to resolve them. His "gambling" is the gesture by which he acknowledges his ignorance, a gesture which paradoxically proves his superior wisdom. For wisdom, according to Bridoye, consists of a man's learning that he is a fool, that all men are fools. It is by his abdication of sanity, by his systematic *déraisonnement*, that Bridoye has access to truths which are inaccessible to reason. He represents that state of "appetitive unknowing", that *docta ignorantia* for which knowledge aims and finds fulfillment:

> Conjecturallement je refererois cestuy heur de jugement en l'aspect benevole des cieulx et faveur des Intelligences motrices, les quelles, en contemplation de la simplicité et affection syncere du juge Bridoye, qui soy deffiant de son savoir... se recommenderoit humblement à Dieu le juste juge, invocqueroit à son ayde la grace celeste... et, par ce sort, exploreroit son decret et bon plaisir; ... par sort estre, en anxieté et doubte des humains, manifestée la volunté divine (44).

If the philosophic and literary values of the quest for truth diverged with the "earthly estates" (who addressed themselves solely to the problem of judgment), it is with Bridoye that these lines converge again. His "inspired gambling" is, to be sure, a philosophic phenomenon. It teaches a lesson which is very similar to that of the Abbaye de Thélème (G, 52-57), an episode which can only be understood by remembering that Will was, in the Renaissance, less a rational than an "appetitive" function.[13] FAY CE QUE VOULDRAS — follow your desires, for they are not prey to the "fraulde du Calumniateur infernal" (TL, 44) as reason is and as are the institutions established by reason and tradition. The desire for good is a natural appetite in man, god-given, and it is by following his appetites that man is led back to divine truths.

But Bridoye's "inspired gambling" has, at the same time, literary implications. It is another defense and illustration of inspiration, and inspiration is by its source both a philosophic and a literary phenomenon. Folly had, from its first mention in chapters thirty-seven and thirty-eight, been praised as a superior judge, but equally important, it had been *praised*. The new freedom proclaimed had been a verbal freedom as well as a philosophic one and had stimulated unrestrained and joyful verbal creation. The mere mention of madness had called forth the spectacular "Blason de Triboulet" (38) and with it the *Tiers Livre* was renewed creatively as well as philosophically. Reason had threatened to stop the quest and end the *Tiers Livre* — a defeat for the writer-as-writer as well as for the philosophic quest undertaken by his characters. It is Bridoye's revindication of the rights of madness which justifies Rabelais as well as Panurge and encourages them both to continue their quest for the Word.

The madness that Bridoye praises is neither Bacchic nor Apollonian nor poetic nor amorous. He only affirms in general the superiority of the appetitive over the rational as a mode of cognition. It now remains to be decided which form of madness shall prevail, that of the Apollonian Pantagruel or of the Bacchic Panurge. It was the dialogue between them which generated the *Tiers Livre* and sustained it for many pages. That dialogue had been set aside to explore the relative merits of wisdom and folly. But with

---

[13] Per Nykrog, "Thélème, Panurge et la Dive Bouteille," *Revue d'Histoire Littéraire de la France*, 65 (1965), 385-397, argues this very convincingly, in order to re-evaluate the meaning of the Abbaye de Thélème and of the quest.

Bridoye's affirmation of the superiority of folly, it is to Pantagruel and Panurge and their friendship that the *Tiers Livre* returns.

The consultation with Folly incarnate, Triboulet (45-47) brings the book back to the format of the oracular consultants, with the difference that here the two friends rely on madness rather than reason to interpret the oracle. Panurge and Pantagruel face Triboulet with new vigor and confidence, for both have felt that Bridoie was describing and defending their particular form of madness. The contest between them in this consultation is hence more energetic and more joyful than any of the others. Yet, the problem of truth is not resolved. This final consultation stands in ironic contrast to Bridoye, for his assertion that folly is superior to reason as an interpreter proves itself, in practice, to be worthless. Folly itself is liable to two divergent interpretations, as Panurge and Pantagruel prove in chapter forty-six when they, as they always have done, "diversement interpretent les parolles de Triboulet." And thus, truth remains to the very end of the *Tiers Livre* as it had stood at the beginning — buried and veiled by its *dédoublement* in the two conflicting interpretations which Panurge and Pantagruel propound. For the truth that Panurge seeks is unattainable. And knowledge remains a *problem*, "un problème insoluble," as Thaumaste had said it was nearly fifteen years before.

We must compare the quest of the *Tiers Livre* to the dilemma that Gargantua faced in 1532 when he could not decide whether to weep for the death of his wife or rejoice in the birth of his son (P, 3). That, too, was "un problème insoluble" and Gargantua might have multiplied arguments to infinity. His dilemma could not be *resolved*, but it was *dissolved* — by life itself, by that instinctive striving which makes men live and love life, makes them father children and write books when it is folly to do so. And thus it is with the *Tiers Livre*. Panurge and Pantagruel might have gone on forever, but Panurge finally drowns out the argumentation. He drowns out even the problems of truth and knowledge — by simply affirming that they will *go on*. Panurge's victory had been forecast by Triboulet's entry on the scene carrying a bottle, Bacchus' emblem. Panurge seizes on that bottle as clear proof, not that his wife will be a drunkard as Pantagruel insists, but rather that the quest must continue. The bottle is to him a clear imperative that they should leave the land and set sail on uncharted waters, toward

Bacchus' own oracle, the oracle of all oracles, "la dive Bouteille." (47) And Pantagruel capitulates. And the *Quart Livre* is born.

Yet Pantagruel participates in Panurge's victory even as he is defeated, for it is unthinkable to Panurge that he should undertake the sea voyage alone. Even though it is he who generates this new quest, he still sees himself as the follower rather than the leader — to Pantagruel, he will play not Eneas but Achates, "...un Damis et compagnon en tout le voyage" (47). For the Bacchic Panurge is the feminine principle in the "marriage" with the Apollonian Pantagruel and he instinctively relies on his mentor's direction. Pantagruel, the Governor, will continue to do in the *Quart Livre* what he has done in the *Tiers Livre*, guide and direct Panurge's quest. It is the task of the Apollonian principle to organize and restrain Bacchus' creative energy, to give it form and order. Without Pantagruel, these books could not have been written, nor could the quest be sustained, and he participates just as fully in the victory of creation as does the Bacchic flood which overwhelms him.

The dynamics of their friendship are expressed by the praise of the "Pantagruélion" which concludes the *Tiers Livre* (49-52). If the plant interprets the emblem *festina lente*,[14] Panurge and Pantagruel may be seen as each reflecting one term of this oxymoron. Panurge is the "hurrying," the plant's unreflective creative energy. Pantagruel, to the contrary, is the "slowness," nature's power to conserve its energy, to guide and direct it so that it can be used to best advantage. Together the two friends represents the opposites of nature and of human nature, of heaven and of earth, the two opposing gods of art — in eternal conflict yet eternally harmonious. Their spiritual and creative marriage "...in like manner as procreation is dependent upon the duality of the sexes, involv(es) perpetual conflicts with only periodically intervening reconciliations."[15] The *Tiers Livre* is one of their most unusual children.

---

[14] See Chapter I, pp. 46-51.
[15] Nietzsche, p. 21.

CHAPTER V

ORPHEUS AND ANTIPHYSIE:
THE QUEST PERILOUS

> Physis (c'est Nature) en sa première portée enfanta Beaulté et Harmonie sans copulation charnelle, comme de soy mesmes est grandement feconde et fertile.
>
> Antiphysie, laquelle de tout temps est partie adverse de Nature, incontinent eut envie sus cestuy tant beau et honorable enfantement; et au rebours enfanta Amodunt et Discordance par copulation de Tellumon. Ilz avoient la teste sphaerique et ronde entierement, comme un ballon; ...Les aureilles avoient hault enlevées, grandes comme aureilles d'asne; les oeilz hors la teste...les pieds ronds comme pelottes, les braz et mains tournez en arriere vers les espaules. Et cheminoient sus leurs testes, continuellement faisant la roue, cul sus teste, les pieds contremont.
>
> Et...Antiphysie louoit et s'efforçoit prouver que la forme de ses enfans plus belle estoit et advenente que des enfans de Physis...
>
> (QL, 32)

The myth of Physis and Antiphysie has rightly been designated as the quintessence of Rabelais's moral and philosophical attitudes.[1] It is a compelling expression of what we know to be his *credo*, one that he enunciated with Thelema, one that is explicit

---

[1] See, for example, Stanley Eskin, "Physis and Antiphysie: The Idea of Nature in Rabelais and Calcagnini," *Comparative Literature*, 14 (1962), 167-173.

throughout these four books — that nature and human nature are good and that the desire for Good is a natural appetite in man. What is evil and perverse derives from Antiphysie and her institutions, from the rhetoric by which she convinces man that ugliness and distortion are truer than Truth. The basis of the satire of the *Quart Livre,* as of the other three books, stems from this *credo,* for one after another the frauds perpetuated by Antiphysie are exposed and attacked.

It is above all the abuses of religion which are the object of Rabelais's most vehement castigation, and they are depicted as Quaresmeprenant and the Andouilles are depicted — as suppressions and perversions of Appetite. For since the desire for God is a natural appetite in man, to subvert appetite is to cut man off from Him. A religious practice whose effect is to alienate man from God is truly, diabolically evil, and this word *evil* must be taken in its fullest sense. It is of utmost significance to the meaning of the *Quart Livre* that Christ is associated with Pan, the pagan god of nature (28). Pan-Physis is pronounced dead, nature is dead, God is dead. The *Quart Livre* is, in a very real sense, Rabelais's *Inferno.* Each *escale* represents a crime against Pan and, as in Dante's voyage, the crimes get progressively more serious, the monsters more demonic. The *Quart Livre,* too, moves ever downward toward an unspeakable Ninth Circle.

However, Rabelais's relationship to Physis and Antiphysie is not as clear-cut as it would seem on the surface. For the "philosopher of nature" commits his thought to words and writes fictions — and language and fiction are the tools of Antiphysie. It is important that Physis and her children are not described in the myth; their reality is so intense and so powerful that words are both inadequate and unnecessary. Antiphysie, to the contrary, has no reality apart from words. She creates her children from nothingness, a void to which she gives form and shape only by language. And only by language can she convince us of their reality. She is, in sum, a fiction-maker and as such she has François Rabelais as her disciple. He uses words exactly as she does, to "enfante Amodunt et Discordance," to create monsters and convince us of their reality. It is a paradox of great importance to the *Quart Livre* that in order to criticize Antiphysie, the writer has to emulate her. And how superbly he does so! Bringuenarilles, Papimanes, Andouilles and Quaresmeprenant — his creations surpass her own.

Rabelais also bears an ambivalent relationship to Physis and Antiphysie as a physician, as *Doctor* Rabelais. Indeed, his profession generates the underlying irony of the *Quart Livre*, that its world of the immoderate and the *immonde* is prefaced by the doctor's praise of health and moderation (Prol., '52). For if, on one hand, the *phys*ician is by definition a disciple of Physis, on the other, he does not treat the body in its natural state of health and harmony. To the contrary, the patient which interests the physician is in an unnatural state of disease and deformity. To cure, he must cut into the sick body and do violence to it — as the monsters of the *Quart Livre* are beaten and torn apart, hacked and hewn and even cut into sausage meat. The physician voraciously performs the tasks of Anti-Nature, but paradoxically, he does so in the name of Nature. He operates to locate the center of disease in order to cure it, so that Physis' equilibrium and beauty may be restored and life may begin again.[2]

Moreover, behind these paradoxes stands the primordial one which generates them all, that Physis and Antiphysie are handmaidens as well as enemies to each other. They are each half of the full cycle of Pan. Antiphysie is the cruel winter which precedes spring, the death and destruction that are the condition of creation and resurrection. In the *Quart Livre*, we experience the death of Physis. We move through the nether regions of the mind and of the body. But Physis is present in hell, present by her absence. She is the yardstick against which disease is measured, the goal toward which the writer-philosopher-physician are steadily working.

Many ancient fables embody these secrets of death and regeneration, but the story of Orpheus, above all others, brings them to bear on the mystery of literary creation. To the Renaissance mind, Orpheus was considered the prototype of the divinely inspired poetic teacher.[3] He was thought to embody all four of Plato's

---

[2] It was Mikhail Bakhtin who first explored the ambivalence of the physician in Rabelais's work. See, especially, the discussion of the Hippocratic novel. (*Rabelais and His World*, pp. 355-362.)

[3] See Daniel P. Walker, "Orpheus the Theologian and Renaissance Platonists," esp. 100-102.

divine furors: both the son of Apollo and a priest of Bacchus, he descended into hell for Love's sake and recounted his voyage in poetry and song. However, of the four, the struggle in him between Apollonian clarity and Bacchic darkness dominated. Orpheus' voyage to the underworld ended with his flaying and dismemberment by the Bacchantes in a terrible Dionysian rite, and in chapter fifty-five of the *Quart Livre*, Pantagruel offers this vision of the torn poet:

> Car après que les femmes Threisses eurent Orpheus mis en pieces, elles jecterent sa teste et sa lyre dans le fleuve Hebrus. Icelles par ce fleuve descendirent en la mer Pontique, jusques en l'isle de Lesbos tousjours ensemble sus mer naigeantes. Et de la teste continuellement sortoyt un chant lugubre, comme lamentant la mort de Orpheus...

Here is the most fearful and most archaic emblem of the process and the price of visionary creation, the gods' violent punishment of Orpheus for his act of transgression against nature, for daring to go beyond *imitation* to the *revelation* of divine secrets hidden beneath nature's exterior appearance. The Orphic poet strives to break, pierce, penetrate the veil and, as he is himself part of nature, he must simultaneously experience the pain of the tearing:

> "... it is as if the myth sought to whisper in our ears that wisdom, especially Dionysian wisdom, is an unnatural abomination and that whoever, through his knowledge, plunges nature into an abyss of annihilation, must also experience the dissolution of nature in himself." [4]

Yet at the same time, the crucifiction of Orpheus is a sign of his election by the Apollo, his father. His flaying and dismemberment is an ordeal of purification: "the 'terrestrial' Bacchus must be tortured so that the 'heavenly' Apollo may be crowned." [5] In order to attain the truth and clarity of mind of the great god of Form, the poet must submit to this ordeal. Orpheus — poet, physician, philosopher — must descend into darkness and disease and he must tear from his own torn body a new child of light.

---

[4] Nietzsche, *The Birth of Tragedy*, p. 75.
[5] Wind, *Pagan Mysteries*, p. 173. See his Chapter 11, pp. 171-176 for a discussion of the relationship between Apollo and Bacchus.

Orpheus descends into Antiphysie in the *Quart Livre*, into a hell that is both personal and cosmic. The physician, the "je" of the Prologue is omnipresent on this voyage, and his purpose in undertaking it is to "cure" himself as well as the world.[6] He is omnipresent, but he is strangely silent in face of the monsters encountered on each *escale*. For two other voices speak for him, two voices who enact the struggle in him, as in Orpheus, between Apollonian clarity and Bacchic darkness.

As in the *Third Book*, Pantagruel embodies the Apollonian temptation in the writer while Panurge is the Bacchic voice. However, unlike the *Tiers Livre*, it is Pantagruel who is associated here with Physis; Panurge has become the disciple of Antiphysie. This is not due to a change in their character, but rather to the fact that they are in the underworld where the relationship between them is reversed. Panurge is instinct, the spontaneous response to what is immediate — and what is immediate in the *Quart Livre* is Antiphysie. Panurge embodies her taste for speech and fantasy. As intellect, spirit, Pantagruel, to the contrary, has no taste for the immediate. He responds instead to an inner idea against which he measures all phenomena encountered. The idea whose torch he holds up in the darkness of the *Quart Livre* is the idea of Physis. Pantagruel is associated in this book with her disdain for irreality, for fantasy, and with her preference for silence.

The conflict between them comes to a climax in the episode where Orpheus' descent into the underworld is cited, the episode of the *Parolles gelées* (55-56). It comes very near the end of the *Quart Livre*, after Quaresmeprenant and the Andouilles, Basché and the Chicquanous, after the *avalleur de moulins* and the *mangeurs du vent*, after all of the terrifyingly wonderful display of the power of Antiphysie. It is as if the creator pauses, with the *Parolles gelées*, to assess what has been at stake throughout the book. He pauses to listen to the dialogue within himself. The episode is, accordingly, divided into two chapters wherein, successively, each of the two voices in him is allowed to speak freely.[7]

---

[6] In the author's Prologue, immediately after the physician inquires into the health of his readers, he launches into the theme: "Medicin, o, gueriz toymesmes."

[7] The best analyses of this episode are: Jean Guiton, "Le mythe des paroles gelées," *Romanic Review*, 31 (1940), 3-15; V. L. Saulnier, "Le Si-

Pantagruel's chapter (55), the "sighting" of the words, is an Apollonian poem to the absence of noise, to noise contained. It takes place on the razor's edge between silence and speech, where the mouth begins to form the word, the pen begins to descend toward the page, but the word is not yet spoken nor is the page sullied. It is the first stirrings of inspiration which approach the writer much as the footsteps of the Muse approach the poet in Valéry's *Les Pas* — shadows of sounds growing ever closer, firmer, more audible.[8] The writer waits with impatience for the act of love that creation is, but he also desires that it should not burst forth. For it is the split second between the idea of creation and creation itself which the writer is cherishing here, that time and place of possibilities so awesome that the writer imagines himself to be divine.

Attentive to the approach of inspiration, Pantagruel speculates as to the nature of the words, and it is by alluding to their divine origin that he begins to speak of them:

> J'ay leu qu'un Philosophe, nommé Petron, estoyt en ceste opinion que feussent plusieurs mondes soy touchans les uns les aultres en figure triangulaire aequilaterale, en la pate et centre des quelz disoit estre le manoir de Verité, et là habiter les Parolles, les Idées, les Exemplaires et protraictz de toutes choses passées et futures: autour d'icelles estre le Siecle. Et en certaines années, par longs intervalles, part d'icelles tomber sus les humains comme catarrhes,...part là rester reservée pour l'advenir, jusques à la consommation du Siecle. (55).[9]

---

lence de Rabelais et le mythe des paroles gelées," in *Ouvrage publié pour le quatrième centenaire...*, pp. 233-247; and Alfred Glauser, *Rabelais créateur*, pp. 277-282.

[8] "Tes pas, enfants de mon silence,
Saintement, lentement placés,
Vers le lit de ma vigilance
Procèdent muets et glacés.
... ...
Ne hâte pas cet acte tendre,
Douceur d'être et de n'être pas,
Car j'ai vécu de vous attendre
Et mon coeur n'était que vos pas."

Paul Valéry, "Le Pas," *Charmes*, in *Oeuvres*, ed. by Jean Hytier (Paris: Gallimard, 1957), I, pp. 120-121.

[9] The word "Siecle" ought not be read here as "century." "Saeculum" has as one of its meanings "eternity" and this is undoubtedly the sense of

The importance of this passage is superlative, for here the nature of the quest is discussed and its object, the *Logos* is identified. As was argued in the Introduction,[10] the quest is placed by Pantagruel in a Platonic context — he clearly conceives of it as a voyage to the world of Ideas where the Forms, the Exemplars reside. But Plato never placed "Parolles" in the Plain of Truth. Rabelais's source for this passage is rather Plutarch, *De Oraculorum Defectu* (22), who used the word *logoi* and who, as he cited Petron, established these entities as co-existent with Ideas in the Intelligible Place. Yet this word *logoi* is subject to more than one translation and more than one interpretation.[11] It is of capital importance that Rabelais unhesitatingly conceptualizes the *logoi* as supernal *Words*, that he identifies these Words with Ideas and makes them equal as the objects of knowledge. These are the Words that Pantagruel hopes he will encounter in the Frozen Sea, Words falling from the world of Ideas which, when thawed, will bring truth.

"In the beginning was the Word...", both a passive Word sufficient unto itself and the creative Word from which our world sprang, and Pantagruel shows interest in the *Logos* in both its passive and creative aspects. The "manoir de Verité" is for him, first, the eternal center of eternity, the point toward which all quests move. At the same time, it is the germinating center which itself moves toward the world. Words fall from the plain of truth into a realm where men may see and hear them. In the examples which follow, Pantagruel is concerned with what kind of men have access to the creative *Logos* and how they participate in it.

In the first degree of proximity to the *Logos* is the writer-philosopher: Aristotle, Homer, Plato and Orpheus, the protagonists of

---

[10] See pp. 22-23.
[11] Frank Cole Babbitt translates *logoi* as "accounts". (Plutarch, *Moralia*, Loeb Classical Library, V, p. 417). Jean Guiton refers to a 17th century translation where the word *rationes* is used. ("Le mythe des paroles gelées," 4.) For an explanation of these translations, read Charles H. Kahn, "A New Look at Heraclitus," *American Philosophical Quarterly*, I (1964), 189-209. Kahn discusses in detail the early history of the word, *before* it came to mean the rational faculty of the soul, the Reason of the Universe, or the Word of God as the second person of the Trinity. Kahn's article should hence be read along with scholarship which explores these later Christian attributes of the *Logos*. See, for example: Jaroslav Pelikan, *The Light of the World* (New York: Harper, 1962); and Harry A. Wolfson, "Extradeical and Intradeical Interpretations of Platonic Ideas," *Journal of the History of*

the three anecdotes which Pantagruel cites. The writer-philosopher receives the *Logos* by inspiration, the words come to him "in the air." He receives them, re-creates them, and becomes himself a new "manoir de Verité." The writer-philosopher thus participates in the creative *Logos* by emulating it. His words are like the Divine Words themselves, autonomous, gifted with life by the divine breath: "...parolles...voltigeantes, volantes, moventes et par consequent animées."

It is the second degree away from the *Logos* which is more problematic and which is the theme of the anecdote of Plato's Frozen Words — the relationship between the writer-philosopher and his reader. For while the poet has an inborn affinity with the *Logos,* that affinity lessens as the hierarchy descends. The problem which confronts the inspired writer is, first, to express his intuitions in their integrity and second, express them so that they may be understood by those whom he wishes to teach. Plato's doctrine of words expresses this double problem of communication and of understanding:

> D'adventaige Antiphanes disoit la doctrine de Platon es parolles estre semblable, lesquelles en quelque contrée, on temps du fort hyver, lors que sont proferées, gelent et glassent à la froydeur de l'air, et ne sont ouyes. Semblablement ce que Platon enseignoyt es jeunes enfans, à peine estre d'iceulx entendu lors que estoient vieulx devenuz. (55)

Perhaps no other single metaphor in the *Quart Livre* is as expressive of Pantagruel's concerns as this one is. He is always associated with the sense of the limits of language that this anecdote expresses, that Thaumaste expressed so many years before when he said that there were "...matieres...tant ardues que les parolles humaines ne (sont) suffisantes à les expliquer..." (P, 18). For words deform thought as they express it. They cannot by their nature express verities which are eternally fixed, since our speech is derived from the world of change and transmutation. Thus, Pantagruel prefers Physis' silence, a silence which expresses both his disdain for human *baragouin* at the same time as it reflects his understanding of nature's deepest truths: "...taciturnité de congnoissance (est) symbole..." (CL, 19).

At the same time as he disdains speech, Pantagruel is concerned, as Plato was, with forcing language to capture somehow the deep reality of things. From Medamothi (2) onward, Pantagruel always strives to give expression to the inexpressible and communicate it to other men. He wants to derive, so to speak, "(une)...maniere de sçavoir nouvelles...des pays estrangiers et loingtains" (3), news from countries such as Medamothi which exist nowhere. And from Medamothi onward, Pantagruel's solution is as Plato's was — to use frozen words, myths which express *via* all the grotesque paraphernalia of Antiphysie, the deepest truths of nature.

Pantagruel is the myth-maker of the *Quart Livre*. He repeatedly directs our attention to the symbolic value of each *escale*, to the truth which lies buried beneath the facade of grotesque *drôlerie*. Often he explicates the symbolism, as he interpreted the death of Pan to be the death of Christ (28), as he used the myth of Physis and Antiphysie to explain Quaresmeprenant. But more frequently, he does not explicate, he only suggests a deeper meaning without stating it.[12] For "the lips of wisdom are sealed save to the ears of understanding."[13] Those who cannot understand will never understand. Those, to the contrary, who have an inborn affinity with truth, or who acquire it with age, will intuit the meaning of the myth in a flash of silent understanding.

The allusion to Orpheus which concludes this chapter continues the speculations related to Plato's doctrine of Frozen Words. Indeed, it was felt by the Renaissance that Orpheus was the parent of such speech and that Plato learned it from him: "...Orpheus interwove the mysteries of his doctrines with the texture of fables and covered them with a poetic veil, in order that anyone reading his hymns would think them to contain nothing but the sheerest tales and trifles."[14] He showed only the "crust of the mysteries to

---

[12] The whole episode of the Chiquanous (12-16), for example, comes to rest on the strange spectacle of the monk "baillé par le coul" because he had "desrobé les ferremens de la messe." "Voila, dist Epistemon, parlé en terrible allegorie" (16). The episode of Messer Gaster concludes similarly, with the anecdote of the "sureau sauvage" which hints at hidden meanings. See below, pp. 114-115.

[13] Hermetic aphorism. See: *The Kybalion* (Chicago: Yogi Publication Society, 1908), p. 15.

[14] Wind, *Pagan Mysteries*, p. 18.

the vulgar, while reserving the marrow of the true sense for higher and more perfect spirits."[15]

The Orphic doctrine of the "poetic veiling of truth" is implicit here, but what is stressed is, to the contrary, the price paid by the poet for the "unveiling," the thawing of nature's frozen words. Orpheus is the dark side of Homer, the dark side of Plato. His words do not fly through the air, they issue from his decapitated head and they lament his death in a "chant lugubre." For the poet's contact with the absolute shatters his being, scatters the members of his body to the four winds. The point of entry into heaven, as Dante understood, is the deepest point in Hell. Pantagruel hopes that they have reached that point in the Frozen Sea, the center of the circle whose circumference is nowhere. And finally, he is afraid.[16]

Chapter fifty-six, Panurge's chapter, forms a sudden and sharp contrast to the seriousness and to the reflective nature of Pantagruel's chapter. Panurge, the Bacchic principle, is the unreflective side of the writer, the side of him which experiences creation as an instinctual drive. Whereas Pantagruel signals the "coming of inspiration," Panurge is the impatience in the writer to precipitate its arrival. He is the writer's impatience to actualize the shadows of sounds which approach him, write them down on the page, see what they are. To speak of voices from heaven, even to hear them, is all very well, but Panurge insists that the Word be made Flesh:

> Mais en pourrions nous veoir quelqu'une. Me soubvient avoir leu que, l'orée de la montaigne en laquelle Moses receut la loy des Juifz, le peuple voyoit les voix sensiblement. (56)

And Pantagruel, with the gesture of a king, throws them down on the deck.

"Voix sensibles" is the key to the nature of Panurge's words. They do not appeal to the mind, but to the ear and to the eye and they confound the data of these senses — sounds are given color, colors are given voice. Panurge does not ask of language that it *mean*, but only that it *be*; he enjoys it as pure *baragouin*. Words

---

[15] *Ibid.*, p. 17.
[16] The first words spoken in Chapter 56 are those of the pilot to Pantagruel: "Seigneur, de rien ne vous effrayez."

are to him objects, toys to be played with, pushed and pulled this way and that, marvelous toys that grow, change shape and become new creatures to be heard and seen and savoured. It has been suggested more than once that his *parolles dégelées* praise the objective value of words.[17] We suggest that, objectively, they have no value at all. Objectively, they are only "*flatus vocis* et cliquetis de mots...matière sonore, sonorité fugitive."[18]

From the beginning, from his meeting with Pantagruel (P, 9), Panurge has always been associated with *parolles dégelées*, with free verbal play, verbal creation, sounds, catalogues, neologisms — with all the kinds of *baragouin* that are displayed in Rabelais's work. Panurge is the "anatomist" of language, the disciple of Antiphysie, who does to words what the physician does to the body, dissects them, breaks them down into their most primitive components in order to find the life-center. And when he reaches the heart of language, he finds no meaning there, no secret doctrine. His words do not originate in heaven; to the contrary, Panurge reveals the origin of speech to be in the animal. His is "food and beast" language,[19] the cries and groans of devouring, of copulation, of birth and death which can generate in us only the primitive passions attached to the animal — joy of life and terror of pain and death.

It is with these two passions, joy and fear, that Panurge is associated in the *Quart Livre*. His first response to the dissolution of nature and of language is always fear — crude, brute, animal fear. But his second reaction is always unrestrained, almost hysterical joy at the forms and colors and shapes that languages takes on when it is freed of the burden of carrying meaning. And, paradoxically, fear and joy are expressed simultaneously by the primitive anti-language that Panurge uses. In the tempest scene (18-24), his cries and shrieks express both the terror of language and the joy

---

[17] This is the opinion of Jean Guiton, "Le Mythe des paroles gelées," and of Leo Spitzer, "Rabelais et les rabelaisants." Spitzer says that in this episode, the writer displays language's "caractère objectif et fixe, transcendant l'individu, subsistant à l'état latent en lui, toujours susceptible d'être actualisé par lui." (p. 403)

[18] Spitzer, "Le prétendu réalisme," 145. The full quotation is given in our Introduction, p. 16.

[19] See the quotation from Henry Miller's *Colossus of Maroussi*, p. 13.

of it. In Chapter fifty-six terror and joy are expressed simultaneously by the contrast between the "color" of the words and the reaction they elicit. The words evoke a dreadful spectacle. They tell of struggle and of death, torture and dismemberment, they are "parolles sanglantes," "parolles horrificques," — cries of pain bubbling from slit throats. It is this spectacle of Antiphysie, her destruction of nature, that causes Panurge and the others to rejoice.

All rejoice except Pantagruel. It is a fact too little noticed that his attitude toward the Frozen Words does a total *volte-face*. His interest in the words, so intense in Chapter fifty-five, vanishes and is replaced by utter disdain and distrust. For the words are not what he hoped they would be, they are not words coming from the "manoir de Verité." They are only *baragouin* of the kind that he has disdained and distrusted all through the *Quart Livre*. They tell a story which, like so many other stories in this book, has monsters for protagonists, monsters who, like so many others, are engaged in a battle. To Pantagruel, this battle is just one more tale of sound and fury which signifies nothing at all.

Pantagruel disdains these thawed words because they are deceptive, because they are cheap and ephemeral, a *feu d'artifice* which bursts and leaves only darkness when it has passed. And he expresses his criticisms of language explicitly. To Panurge, who wants more and more words, Pantagruel admonishes:

> ...donner parolles (est) acte des amoureux. Vendez m'en doncques, disoit Panurge. —C'est acte de advocatz, respondit Pantagruel, vendre parolles. Je vous vendroys plus tost silence et plus cherement... (56)

Pantagruel has a similar exchange with another member of the group who is as enamoured of the thawed words as Panurge, who also wants to pick them up, play with them, pickle them and keep them forever:

> Je vouloys quelques motz de gueule mettre en reserve dedans de l'huille, comme l'on garde la neige et la glace, et entre du feurre bien nect. Mais Pantagruel ne le voulut, disant estre follie faire reserve de ce dont jamais l'on n'a faulte et que tous jours on a en main comme sont motz de gueule entre tous bons et joyeulx Pantagruelistes.

The "Je" who is speaking is, of course Alcofribas himself and it is significant that when the author-narrator intervenes, he allies himself with Panurge. The side of him which revels in speech and fantasy is powerful indeed. But it is also significant that his voice is silenced almost as soon as it has committed itself. For the glorious *tintamarre* of the thawed words passes and abruptly the group is left cold and empty-handed. Panurge and Frère Jean become embroiled in a bitter and confusing argument and suddenly Panurge is persuaded to Pantagruel's point of view. The entire edifice of this chapter — this incredible display of the power of language and the love of it — comes to rest on *Panurge*'s rejection of the thawed words. Suddenly he desires what Pantagruel desires, the Frozen Word, the Word which when thawed will bring truth:

> Pleust à Dieu que icy, sans plus avant proceder, j'eusse le mot de la dive Bouteille!

Although it is the most compelling, the most quintessential expression of Rabelais's ambivalence toward language and toward literary creation, the episode of the *Parolles Gelées* is not unique in the themes it develops. It is, however, unique in its conclusion. Whatever moral superiority Pantagruel has had over Panurge, it has always before been the Bacchic principle which triumphed and his triumph assured the generation of new words and new quests. Here the Apollonian principle has the final word, language and fantasy are rejected in favor of wordlessness. And it is Pantagruel's victory which determines the peculiar climate of the end of the *Quart Livre*. One after another islands of fantasy are refused as Chaneph (63-65) and Ganabin (66) are refused. The book is becalmed, it drowses, all is wrapped in a mantle of silence. One after another eulogies of silence are offered — admirable episodes, yet worrisome, oblique, unfulfilling. For the wind of Bacchic inspiration has been banished and we, like the *équipe*, experience boredom and anxiety as we await its return. We await the return of Bacchus who will "haulser le temps,"[20] and banish the silence and

---

[20] This episode does in fact end with Pantagruel's praise of Bacchus as the "winged one":

> Ne sçavez vous que jadis les Amycleens sus tous Dieux reveroient et adoroient le noble pere Bacchus, et le nommoient *Psila* en

sterility which Pantagruel's victory in the *Parolles gelées* has bequeathed to the voyage.

The episode of Messer Gaster (57-62) stands between the *Parolles gelées* and "Maniere de Haulser le Temps" (63-65) — it is a final verbal *sursaut* before the heavy silence sets in. The Gaster episode is one of the longest in the *Quart Livre*, and is of singular importance to the book. It relates directly to the problems of language and literary creation as they were elaborated in the *Paroles gelées*, and it puts these problems back into the larger context of the central dilemma with which the *Quart Livre* is struggling — the problematic relationship between Physis and Antiphysie.

Gaster, God of the Belly and of Appetite, is associated fully and completely with both Physis' disdain for speech and Antiphysie's verbal creation. Like Physis, he is a god of silence, he has no ears to hear and he does not speak: "...ainsi Gaster sans aureilles feut créé, comme en Candie le simulachre de Juppiter estoit sans aureilles. Il ne parle que par signes" (57). But at the same time Gaster is the enemy of silence. He is the imperious god of language, "le Dieu Ventripotent" who commands that all creatures open their mouths, which is to *talk* as well as to eat. In the *Tiers Livre* we were told that when the children in Psammeticus' experiment broke their life-long silence, they shouted out Gaster's word: *Becus*, bread! (TL, 19). And in chapter fifty-seven of the *Quart Livre*, this theme is given a new twist. Here we are told that Gaster has the power to put this human word into the mouths of mute animals and caused them to elaborate that word into the artful language of poetry and song: "Les corbeaulx, les gays, les papeguays, les estourneaulx, il rend poëtes, les pies il faict poëtrides, et leurs aprent languaige humain proferer, parler, chanter. Et tout pour la trippe!"

The most loquacious apostles of Messer Gaster, human or animal, are without a doubt the Gastrolatres and their festival in his honor is the high point of this episode. It is the festival of the

---

propre et convenente denomination? *Psila*, en langue doricque, signifie aesles. Car comme les oyzeaulx par ayde de leurs aesles volent hault en l'air legierement, ainsi par l'ayde de Bacchus (c'est le bon vin friant et delicieux) sont hault eslevez les espritz des humains, leurs corps evidentement alaigriz, et assouply ce que en eulx estoit terrestre." (65)

gaping mouth that eats and talks. In emulation of their creative mother, Antiphysie, the Gastrolatres fashion a monster, Manduce:

> "...une effigie, monstreuse, ridicule, hydeuse et terrible aux petitz enfans...avecques amples, larges, et horrificques maschoueres bien endentelées... lesquelles... l'on faisoit l'un contre l'aultre terrificquement clicquetter..." (59).

Into this gaping mouth are poured page after page of foods, of words which resume all the banquets of the book. All of the foods that have been "eaten" and "talked" in the *Quart Livre* are put once again into the open maw of Manduce and down into Gaster's belly — *Pains, Andouilles, Saulcisses, Boudins, Cervelatz, Saumons, Purées de poys, Beurre frays, Figues, Poires* — all of the adventures of the *Quart Livre* are resumed and consumed in this banquet, *en salmigondin*. [21]

There can be no doubt that the book is praised by this enthusiastic encyclopedia. Manduce and the Gastrolatres represent the positive, Bacchic principle of food and drink and the wondrous table-talk which is the essence of the *Quart Livre*. But at the same time, the Gastrolatres are condemned, "poys et charge inutile de la Terre" (58). And finally, the whole banquet is repudiated by Gaster. With a silent gesture of mockery, the king sits on his "throne" — *Totus homo fit excrementum*. [22] He degrades the whole festival — with all its foods and all its words — by reducing it to a mound of fecal matter.

For behind all the hullaballoo of this episode, Gaster's form has stood in silent criticism of language. Appetite may generate words, but it, itself, speaks beyond words, it decimates all justification for speech. As a physical need, Appetite does not require speech: "...l'estomach affamé n'a poinct d'aureilles, il n'oyt goutte. Par signes, gestes et effectz serez satisfaicts..." (63). Panurge first stated this theme in 1532 when he met Pantagruel, and time has

---

[21] Salmigondin is defined by Cotgrave as "A Hachee; or meat made ordinarily of cold flesh, cut in little pieces, and stewed or boyled on a chafingdish, with crummes of bread, wine, vertuyce, vinegar, sliced Nutmeg and Orange pills." It is also, we remember, the name of the province given to Alcofribas in chapter 32 of the *Pantagruel*, the province which Panurge governs in the *Tiers Livre*.

[22] Hugo, *Shakespeare*, p. 40.

not changed Rabelais's conviction that language is superfluous when the natural drives are in question.

The deceptiveness of language is more serious when Appetite is felt as the hunger for the Good and the Beautiful. As it happened, with the *parolles dégelées,* language threatens to subvert the quest for truth. It is no mistake that the Gastrolatres act out a rite which parodies a religious service, a kind of black mass. For in perverting Appetite, they separate man from God and in this they are diabolical. They perpetuate "...la fraulde du Calumniateur infernal lequel souvent se transfigure en messagier de lumiere par ses ministres... tourne le noir en blanc, faict phantasticquement sembler à l'une et l'aultre partie qu'elle a bon droict..." (TL, 44). Like Bringuenarilles and the "mangeurs du vent," words cause us to eat the wind and take shadows for our meat. Truth is apprehended in silence, truth is silence, and "tout le reste est littérature."

Thus, though speech and silence are present in their plenitude, the episode of Messer Gaster ends by repudiating language. It ends as the *Parolles gelées* had ended, with a praise of the Frozen Word:

> ...le suzeau (sureau) croist, plus canore (sonore) et plus apte au jeu des flustes, en pays on quel le chant des coqs ne sera ouy, ainsi qu'ont escript les anciens sages, scelon le rapport de Theophraste...
>
> Je sçay que aultres ont ceste sentence entendu du suzeau saulvaige, provenent en lieux tant esloignez de villes et villages... sans doubte doist pour flustes et aultres instrumens de musicque estre esleu et preferé au domestique.... Aultres l'ont entendu plus haultement, non selon la lettre, mais allegoricquement scelon l'usaige des Pythagoriens.... (E)n ceste sentence nous enseignent que les gens saiges et studieux ne se doibvent adonner à la musique triviale et vulgaire, mais à la celeste, divine, angelique, plus absconse et de plus loing apportée: scavoir est d'une region en laquelle n'est ouy des coqs le chant. (62)

All the themes of Plato's "doctrine es parolles" are here reiterated. The deepest, most serious truths cannot be expressed directly in speech, they may only be alluded to in symbols and myths. The "bone" of the allegory may be enjoyed for itself, but the wise man does not stop at appearances. He penetrates the outer core and seeks the deep meaning, one that transcends speech and is apprehended in silence, for it comes from the region of silence where the sound of the cock is never heard.

Ganabin (66) is yet another variation on the themes of the *Parolles gelées* and of Gaster. Once again the relative value of speech and silence is debated and the wisdom of literary creation is thrown into question. Ganabin is called "le mons Antiparnasse," and this designation expresses the deep ambivalence that the voyageurs feel toward the island. On one hand, as Parnassus it exercises a great attraction, for Ganabin is said to be the site of "la plus belle fontaine du monde," and we must associate this spring with the "fontaine caballine" that Rabelais called his "unicque enthusaisme" in the prologue to the *Tiers Livre*. Like Bacchus' barrel of wine, this beautiful fountain generates joy, it is a source of thawed words which grow, mutate and become new words, charming and confounding the senses. But on the other hand, that fountain is repudiated by the negative prefix: *Anti*-Parnassus, and by Pantagruel who damns those who drink of it as "voleurs et larrons". He censors these word-men as Gaster censored the Gastrolatres. For all their charm, these words and these wordmen practice a dreadful deception. They subvert and pervert the quest for the Word.

Beuver de la fontaine ou ne pas beuver? This is the question which is debated by the group as they near Ganabin and the arguments rage long and loud. Panurge does not want to stop; as always, he is terrified of language. Frère Jean insists, to the contrary, that they visit Ganabin and see its wonders for themselves. The argument is settled by Pantagruel:

> Je sens ... en mon ame retraction urgente, comme si feust une voix de loing ouye, laquelle me dict que ne y doibvons descendre. Toutes et quantes foys qu'en mon esprit j'ay tel mouvement senty, je me suis trouvé en heur, refusant et laissant la part dont il me retiroit; au contraire en heur pareil me suys trouvé, suivant la part qu'il me poulsoit; et jamais ne m'en repenty.
> —C'est, dist Epistemon, comme le Daemon de Socrates, tant celebré entre les Academicques (66).

Ne pas Beuver! The fountain is refused. Pantagruel will not relent as he had done with the Frozen Words. He will not allow the words to be actualized, only to be again disappointed. The ship passes on.

Nietzsche, who expresses no love for Socrates in *The Birth of Tragedy*, remarks there that his Daemon is a voice of negation.[23] This is certainly true of Apollonian inspiration as Pantagruel exemplifies it. Four "voices in the air" are heard in the *Quart Livre*; all four are associated with Pantagruel and all four are voices of negation: announcing the death of Pan (28); urging the repudiation of language (*Parolles gelées*, "sureau sauvage"); and finally, causing islands of fantasy to be refused, as Chaneph and Ganabin are refused. And we see at last that Pantagruel, the spokesman of Physis, becomes by the very degree of his devotion to her, Antiphysie — denying life and movement, denying words. In his desire for the eternal, Pantagruel is the harbinger of immobility and sterility, of death. What opportunities for creation are rejected by him on Chaneph and Ganabin? What incredible surges of fantasy does he cause Rabelais to stifle in himself?

However, neither Apollo's triumph nor Bacchus' defeat is absolute — the ambiguity of the episode is maintained until the end. They pass by Ganabin, it is true, but they *salute* it, they salute "les Muses de cestuy Mons Antiparnasse". All the guns of all the boats in the convoy are loaded and they fire simultaneously. "Croyez qu'il y eut beau tintamarre!", an explosion which is cousin germane to the gush of the fountain, the bursting of the frozen words, the banquet of the Gastrolatres. This episode marks the acme of Pantagruel's influence and its decline. Silence is dispelled as they salute the Muses of Antiparnasse, and the renewal of the book is announced.

For all of its vulgarity, the final chapter is consistent with the development of the *Quart Livre*. It completes the downward move-

---

[23] "A key to the character of Socrates is presented to us by the surprising phenomenon designated as the 'daimonion' of Socrates. In special circumstances, when his gigantic intellect began to stagger, he got a secure support in the utterances of a divine voice which then spake to him. This voice, whenever it comes, always *dissuades*. In this totally abnormal nature, instinctive wisdom only appears in order to hinder the progress of conscious perception here and there. While in all productive men, it is instinct which is the creatively affirmative force, consciousness only comporting itself critically and dissuasively; with Socrates, it is instinct which becomes critic, it is consciousness which becomes creator — a perfect monstrosity *per defectum!*" (p. 105)

ment of the quest and culminates the struggle between Bacchic darkness and Apollonian clarity of mind, the struggle which has provided the dynamics of this Orphic voyage to the underworld. It is, in fact (although the comparison seems heretical), the equivalent of the last canto of Dante's *Inferno*. The hold, where Panurge had descended in chapter sixty-six, is the lowest point of the book, the ninth circle where the devil resides:

> Agua, men emy! ... tous les Diables sont aujourd'huy de nopces. Tu ne veids oncques tel apprest de bancquet infernal. Voy tu la fumée des cuisines d'Enfer?
> ... ce chat? ... je me donne au Diable si je ne pensoys que feust un Diableteau à poil follet, lequel nagueres j'avois cappiettement happé en tapinois ... dedans la grande husche d'Enfer (67).

As in the *Inferno*, the ninth circle of the *Quart Livre* is both the apex of the cycle of darkness and the beginning of the cycle of light; fear reaches its peak here and fear is dispelled. All of the phenomena of this episode are ambivalent, relating both to death and to life. The attack of the cat Rodilardus is akin to the final movement of the Prologues to *Gargantua* and to the *Tiers Livre*; it is the Bacchic flaying and dismemberment, the death which is the condition of creation. Fecal matter, too, is ambivalent. Panurge "par male paour, se conchia," a gesture of debasement, a symbolic "death," a reduction to inert matter. However, the act of defecation purges as the same time as it debases. Like the flaying, it is a "gay death," it is fertile, it is the dead material out of which new life springs. [24]

Indeed, the final chapter of the *Quart Livre* must be read as a parable of death and regeneration. Its bodily topology is as precise as that of another joyful advent — the birth of Gargantua. Like him, Panurge is created in destruction, in the labyrinth of tripe and fecal matter which twines menacingly around the womb. But, also like Gargantua, Panurge triumphs over death and fear by reversing

---

[24] The reader is referred once again to Mikhail Bakhtin who, throughout *Rabelais and His World*, stresses the ambivalence of the grotesque imagery and actions such as the beatings and scatology in this chapter. See, in particular, Chapter II, pp. 147-150 and Chapter III, pp. 198-213.

the geometry of birth and climbing *up* and out of the ear, of the fearful mouth of hell. And as he emerges into new life, Panurge concludes Rabelais's odyssey in the same way as the child began, with a joyful call to fresh life and further voyages. "A Boire!" cried Gargantua in the beginning. "Beuvons!" shouts Panurge at the end.

This last call to drink [25] affirms that the *Quart Livre* has survived the lands of ice and silence through which it was doomed to pass. The Frozen Word is cracked open now and its precious liqueur drowns out Pantagruel's *Défense de boire*. At last we may drink of Bacchus' wine, enjoy the thawed words freely. "Le mot de la Bouteille" so long sought is found at last. It is the word of the God of wine, as we have always known it would be. And Bacchus' word praises life-as-we-know-it and the word-as-it-is. It is the word made flesh which praises flesh and all its transmutations.

---

[25] Our use of the final "Beuvons" of the *Quart Livre* as "le mot de la dive Bouteille" will be defended in the *Conclusion*.

CONCLUSION

It all began in 1532 when Pantagruel met Panurge on the road to Paris; their meeting is the embryo from which the whole long voyage of these four books was born. Panurge demonstrated there his fantastic talent as a manipulator of words, as a creator of languages — he is the most virtuoso *maître es langues* that the world has ever known. Yet behind his sparkling cascade of *baragouin,* silence also spoke and it spoke loudly; it decimated all justification for words. Panurge came to heed only the speech and Pantagruel, the silence; and they set out together to solve the problem of language which had disturbed their meeting. They set out in search of the *Logos* where speech and silence are melded. They called it "le mot de la dive Bouteille."

We have chosen not to pursue their quest into the *Cinquiesme Livre*[1] because of the questions surrounding its authenticity. Although partisans of the *Fifth Book* have put forth persuasive arguments in their "cautious search for probabilities,"[2] in the end it must be admitted that there can be no final solution until solid, new, scholarly evidence is put forth. Until that time, *Le Cinquiesme Livre* must stand, like so many other Rabelaisian enigmas, balanced between pro and contra arguments of equal plausibility.

---

[1] *Le Cinquiesme et dernier livre des faicts et dicts heroïques du bon Pantagruel, composé par M. Françoys Rabelais, Docteur en Medecine...* (1564) was preceded by *L'Isle Sonnante par M. Françoys Rabelays...* (1562) which consisted of 16 chapters and no prologue.

[2] Greene, *Comic Courage*, p. 100. This book gives a good summary of the arguments for and against the *Cinquiesme Livre*, pp. 100-102. A more detailed exploration is offered by Mallary Masters, *Rabelaisian Dialectic,* pp. 100-109.

Nonetheless, there does appear to be a strong and striking parallelism between the final episode of *Book Five* and the last chapter of the *Quart Livre*. Indeed, as a parable of death and regeneration, this chapter may be read as an *esquisse* of the end of *Le Cinquiesme Livre*. The geometry of the initiatory voyage, and its main symbolism are complete in miniature: the descent downward to the heart of darkness, the symbolic death, the renewal and final rebirth in wine. In the *Quart Livre* also, Panurge is cleansed after his ordeal and sent to "prendre chemise blanche," much as the underground voyagers in *Le Cinquiesme Livre* are clothed in white as a sign of their initiation.

The *Fourth Book* is admittedly far less delicate than the Fifth in its elaboration of these themes, but as *The Golden Ass* of Apuleis reveals, scatology has always had an important role in rituals of initiation. This old masterpiece is a splendid example of the mysterious logic whereby comic, vulgar, bodily voyages culminate in rites of the highest spiritual significance. The final chapters of both the *Quart* and the *Cinquiesme Livres* can be compared to the *Golden Ass*, which also clarifies the tie that binds the two episodes together.

However, this argument may be used just as effectively to sweep aside the *Fifth Book*. For if the voyage is complete symbolically in the last book of certain authenticity, there is no need to rely on what may well be the work of an adroit *pasticheur*. The final "Beuvons" of the *Quart Livre* is just as fully "le mot de la dive Bouteille" as the "Trinch" of the *Cinquiesme Livre* and it has the same significance. It is a cry of exaltation which expresses the overcoming of fear and the restoration of joy and harmony to self and to the world.[3] We do not need to wait until 1564 to hear that cry. It rings out in 1552, at the end of the *Quart Livre*.

And as that word resounds, the ultimate paradox of a series of paradoxes that have surrounded the quest is revealed — that the conversion to a new life takes the form of an ecstatic return to the *old*. The "Beuvons" sends the voyagers back to pursue with new vigor and confidence the endeavors they have always pursued: the quest for a wife and for paternity, for authorship, for creation

---

[3] These remarks paraphrase Masters' interpretation of the Word of the *Fifth Book, ibid.,* p. 63. The whole section "*Homo Bibens*: Contemplative Knowledge of the Dionysian Mysteries", p. 57-67, is pertinent here.

and creativity of all sorts. The end sends the book back to its beginning.

And in the Beginning and in the End was the Word: "Beuveurs tres illustres..." (G, p), "Beuvons" (QL, 67). In the Middle, over and over again, was the Word. When Pantagruel and Panurge first struggled with language and set out "à la poursuite du Mot,"[4] they already possessed the word which they sought. But it urged them to seek again. *Trinch*, Thaumaste! Panurge, *beuvez*! Plunge into the bottomless well where truth lies waiting and drink of it so that the whole cycle may begin again! Rabelais's voyage will turn on its own axis throughout all of time, both sufficient unto itself and pushed by its lacking" to seek its own truth:

> We shall not cease from exploration
> And the end of all our exploring
> Will be to arrive where we started
> And know the place for the first time.[5]

---

[4] Guiton, "Le Mythe des paroles gelées," 9.
[5] T. S. Eliot, "Little Gidding," *The Four Quartets* (New York: Harvest Books, 1943), p. 59.

SELECTED BIBLIOGRAPHY

A. PRIMARY SOURCES

1. RABELAIS

Oeuvres, ed. Abel Lefranc, et al. Paris-Geneva; Champion-Droz, 1913-1965. 7 vols.
Oeuvres complètes, ed. Jacques Boulenger. *Bibliothèque de la Pléiade*. Paris: Gallimard, 1955.
Oeuvres complètes, ed. Pierre Jourda. Paris: Garnier, 1962. 2 vols.
Oeuvres complètes, ed. Jean Plattard. Paris: Société d'Edition "Les Belles Lettres", 1946-48. 5 vols.
Gargantua, ed. Ruth Calder, intro. and comment. M. A. Screech. Geneva: Droz, 1970.
Pantagruel, ed. Robert Marichal. Lyon: Association Générale de l'Internat et du Conseil d'Administration des Hospices Civils, 1935.
Pantagruel, ed. Verdun L. Saulnier. Paris: Droz, 1946.
Le Quart Livre, ed. Robert Marichal. Lille-Geneva: Droz, 1947.
Le Tiers Livre, ed. M. A. Screech. Geneva: Droz, 1964.

2. OTHER

Bergson, Henri. *La Pensée et le mouvant*. Vol. 1 of *Oeuvres complètes d'Henri Bergson*. Geneva: Editions Albert Skira, 1946. 3 vols.
Castiglione, Baldassar. *Book of the Courtier*. Translated by Charles S. Singleton. Garden City, N. Y.: Doubleday, 1959.
Colonna, Francesco. *Le Songe de Poliphile*. Paris: Club des Libraires de France, 1963.
Cusanus, Nicolaus. *Of Learned Ignorance*. Translated by Germain Heron. New Haven: Yale University Press, 1954.
Dante Alighieri. *The Divine Comedy*. Translated by John D. Sinclair. New York: Oxford, 1961. 3 vols.
Du Bellay, Joachim. *La Deffence et illustration de la langue francoyse*. Edition critique par Henri Chamard. Paris: Didier, 1948.
Erasmus, Desiderius. *Essential Works of Erasmus*. Edited by W. T. H. Jackson. New York: Bantam Books, 1965.
Eliot, T. S. *The Four Quartets*. New York: Harvest Books, 1943.
Ficino, Marsilio. *Commentary on the Banquet*. Translated by Sears Jayne. Columbia, Mo.: The University of Missouri Studies, 1944. Vol. 19.

SELECTED BIBLIOGRAPHY 123

Ficino, Marsilio. "Five Questions Concerning the Mind." Translated by Josephine L. Burroughs. In *The Renaissance Philosophy of Man*. Edited by Ernst Cassirer, Paul Oskar Kristeller and John Herman Randall, Jr. Chicago: The University of Chicago Press, 1965, pp. 185-212.
——. *Opera Omnia*. Edited by M. Sancipriano and Paul Oskar Kristeller. Torino: Bottega d'Erasmo, 1959. 2 vols.
Gellius, Aulus. *The Attic Nights*. Trans. by John C. Rolf. Cambridge, Mass.: Harvard University Press, 1960. 3 vols.
Hermes Trismegistus. *Corpus Hermeticum*. Edited by A. D. Nock and A. J. Festugière. Paris: Société d'Edition "Les Belles Lettres", 1945-1954. 4 vols.
Horapollo. *Hieroglyphics*. Trans. by George Boas. New York: Pantheon Books, 1950.
Hugo, Victor. *William Shakespeare*. Vol. 41 of *Oeuvres complètes*. Paris: Albin Michel, 1937.
The Kybalion. Chicago: Yogi Publication Society, 1908.
Lemaire de Belges, Jean. *La Concorde des deux langages*. Edition critique par Jean Frappier. Paris: Droz, 1947.
Montaigne, Michel de. *Oeuvres complètes*. Ed. by Albert Thibaudet & Maurice Rat. Paris: Bibliothèque de la Pléiade, 1967.
Nietzsche, Friedrich. *The Birth of Tragedy*. Translated by William A. Haussmann. Vol. 1 of *The Complete Works of Friedrich Nietzsche*. Edited by Oscar Levy. New York: Russell and Russell, 1964.
Pico della Mirandola, Giovanni. "Oration on the Dignity of Man." Translated by Elizabeth Livermore Forbes. In *The Renaissance Philosophy of Man*. Edited by Ernst Cassirer, Paul Oskar Kristeller and John Herman Randall, Jr. Chicago: The University of Chicago Press, 1965, pp. 223-254.
Plato. *Collected Dialogues including the Letters*. Edited by Edith Hamilton and Huntington Cairns. New York: Pantheon Books, 1961.
Pliny. *Natural History*. Translated by H. Rackham. The Loeb Classical Library. London-Cambridge, Mass.: W. Heinemann, 1938-1963. 10 vols.
Plotinus. *Enneads*. Translated by Stephen Mackenna. The Library of Philosophical Translations. London-Boston: The Medici Society. 1926. 5 vols.
Plutarch. *Moralia*. Trans. by Frank Cole Babbitt. Loeb Classical Library. London: Heinemann, 1936.
Ronsard, Pierre de. *Les Oeuvres*. Edited by Isidore Silver. Chicago: The University of Chicago Press; Paris: Didier, 1966. 7 vols.
Scève, Maurice. *La Délie*. Ed. by I. D. McFarlane. Cambridge, Eng., The University Press, 1966.
Tory, Geofroy. *Champ Fleury*. New York: Johnson reprint, 1970.
Tyard, Pontus de. *Le Solitaire premier*. Edition critique par Silvio Baridon. Lille: Girard; Geneva: Droz, 1950.
Valéry, Paul. *Oeuvres*. Edited by Jean Hytier. *Bibliothèque de la Pléiade*. Paris: Gallimard. 1957. 2 vols.

B. SECONDARY SOURCES

Allen, Don Cameron. "The Rehabilitation of Epicurus and his Theory of Pleasure in the Early Renaissance," *Studies in Philology*, 41 (1944), 1-15.
Auerbach, Erich. "The World in Pantagruel's Mouth," *Mimesis*. Translated by Willard Trask. Garden City, N. J.: Doubleday, 1957, pp. 229-249.

Bakhtin, Mikhail. *Rabelais and His World.* Translated by Helene Iswolsky. Cambridge, Mass.: M.I.T. Press, 1968.
Beaujour, Michel. *Le Jeu de Rabelais.* Paris: Editions de l'Herne, 1969.
Beauvoir, Simone de. *Le Deuxième Sexe.* Paris: Gallimard, 1949.
Blau, Joseph L. *The Christian Interpretation of the Cabala in the Renaissance.* New York: Columbia University Press, 1944.
Boulenger, Jacques. *Rabelais.* Paris: Editions Colbert, 1942.
———. *Rabelais à travers les âges.* Paris: Le Divan, 1925.
Bowen, Barbara. *The Age of Bluff: Paradox and Ambiguity in Rabelais and Montaigne.* Urbana: University of Illinois Press, 1962.
———. "Rabelais and the Comedy of the Spoken Word," *Modern Language Review,* 63 (1968), 575-580.
Brault, Gerard J. " 'Une Abysme de Science': On the Interpretation of Gargantua's Letter to Pantagruel," *Bibliothèque d'Humanisme et Renaissance,* 28 (1966), 615-632.
Bréhier, Emile. "Images plotiniennes et images bergsoniennes," *Etudes Bergsoniennes,* 2 (1949), 105-128.
———. *La Philosophie de Plotin.* Paris: Boivin, 1928.
Brown, Harcourt. "Ideas and Rabelais," *Bucknell Review,* 9 (1960), 177-186.
Butor, Michel and Hollier, Denis. *Rabelais ou c'était pour rire.* Paris: Larousse, 1972.
Carpenter, Nan Cooke. *Rabelais and Music.* Chapel Hill: University of North Carolina Press, 1954.
Carré, Meyrick H. *Realists and Nominalists.* London and New York: Oxford University Press, 1946.
Cassirer, Ernst. *The Individual and the Cosmos.* Trans. by Mario Domandi. New York: Barnes & Noble, 1963.
———. *Language.* Vol. 1 of *The Philosophy of Symbolic Forms.* Trans. by Ralph Manheim. New Haven: Yale University Press, 1953-57. 3 vols.
Cassirer, Ernst; Kristeller, Paul Oskar; and Randall, John Herman, Jr. *The Renaissance Philosophy of Man.* Chicago: University of Chicago Press, 1965.
Cave, Terence. "Ronsard as Apollo: Myth, Poetry and Experience in a Renaissance Sonnet-cycle," *Yale French Studies,* 47 (1972), 76-89.
———. "Ronsard's Bacchic Poetry: from the *Bacchanales* to the *Hymne de l'autonne,*" *Esprit Créateur,* 10, no. 2 (1970), 104-116.
Chamard, Henri. *Histoire de la Pléiade.* Paris: Didier, 1939-1940. 4 vols.
Clement, Nemours H. *The Influence of the Arthurian Romances on the Five Books of Rabelais.* Berkeley: University of California Press, 1926.
Clements, Robert J. *Picta Poesis: Literary and Humanistic Theory in Renaissance Emblem Books.* Rome: Edizioni di Storia e Letteratura, 1960.
Clouzot, Henri. "Marguerite de Navarre et Rabelais," *Revue du Seizième Siècle,* 19 (1932-33), 300-301.
Coleman, Dorothy. "The Prologues of Rabelais," *Modern Language Review,* 62 (1967), 407-419.
———. *Rabelais: A Critical Study in Prose Fiction.* London: Cambridge University Press, 1971.
Colie, Rosalie L. *Paradoxia Epidemica: The Renaissance Tradition of Paradox.* Princeton: Princeton University Press, 1966.
Colish, Marcia. *The Mirror of Language: A Study in the Medieval Theory of Knowledge.* New Haven & London: Yale University Press, 1968.

Curtius, Ernst. *European Literature and the Latin Middle Ages.* Trans. by Willard Trask. New York: Pantheon Books, 1953.

Dannenfeldt, Karl H. "Egypt and Egyptian Antiquities in the Renaissance," *Studies in Philology,* 6 (1959), 7-27.

Defaux, Gerard. *Pantagruel et les Sophistes.* The Hague: Nijhoff, 1973.

Delaruelle, Louis. "Ce que Rabelais doit à Erasme et à Budé," *Revue d'Histoire Littéraire de la France,* 11 (1904), 220-262.

Derrett, J. Duncan M. "Rabelais' Legal Learning and the Trial of Bridoie," *Bibliothèque d'Humanisme et Renaissance,* 25 (1963), 111-171.

Dieckmann, Liselotte. *Hieroglyphics: The History of a Literary Symbol.* St. Louis: Washington University Press, 1970.

Diéguez, Manuel de. *Rabelais par lui-même.* Paris: Editions du Seuil, 1960.

Ehrmann, Jacques. "La Temporalité dans l'oeuvre de Rabelais," *French Review,* 37 (1963), 188-199.

Ellman, Richard. *James Joyce.* New York: Oxford Univ. Press, 1959.

Engstrom, Alfred G. "A few comparisons and contrasts in the word-craft of Rabelais and James Joyce," *Renaissance and Other Studies in Honor of W. L. Wiley.* Edited by George Daniel. Chapel Hill: University of North Carolina Press, 1968, 65-82.

Eskin, Stanley G. "Mythic Unity in Rabelais," *PMLA,* 79 (1964), 548-553.

———. "Physis and Antiphysie: The Idea of Nature in Rabelais and Calcagnini," *Comparative Literature,* 14 (1962), 167-173.

Esslin, Martin. *Bertolt Brecht.* New York and London: Columbia Univ. Press, 1969.

Febvre, Lucien. *Le Problème de l'incroyance au XVIe siècle: La Religion de Rabelais.* Paris: Michel, 1942.

Festugière, A.-J. *La Philosophie de l'amour de Marsile Ficin et son influence sur la littérature française au XVIe siècle.* Paris: Vrin, 1941.

———. *La Révélation d'Hermès Trismégiste.* Paris: Gabalda, 1949-1953. 4 vols.

Foulet, Alfred. "Les Aventures des gens curieux," *Romanic Review,* 54 (1963), 3-5.

Frame, Donald. "The Impact of Frère Jean on Panurge in Rabelais's *Tiers Livre,*" *Renaissance and Other Studies in Honor of W. L. Wiley.* Edited by George Daniel. Chapel Hill: University of North Carolina Press, 1968, 83-91.

Franchet, Henri. *Le Poète et son oeuvre d'après Ronsard.* Paris: Champion, 1922.

France, Anatole. *Rabelais.* Paris: Calmann-Lévy, 1928.

Françon, Marcel. "A note on the word 'symbolisation' in the *Tiers Livre,*" *Modern Language Review,* 55 (1960), 84-85.

———. *Autour de la lettre de Gargantua à son fils (Pantagruel, 8).* Cambridge, Mass.: Harvard University Press, 1964.

Frautschi, R. L. "The *Enigme en prophétie* and the question of authorship," *French Studies,* 17 (1963), 331-339.

Friedrich, Hugo. *Montaigne.* Trans. by Robert Rovini. Paris: Gallimard, 1968.

Frohock, W. M. "Panurge as Comic Character," *Yale French Studies,* 23 (1959), 71-76.

Garapon, Robert. *La Fantaisie verbale et le comique dans le théâtre français du moyen âge au XVIIe siècle.* Paris: Colin, 1957.

Gebhart, Emile. *Rabelais, la renaissance et la réforme.* Paris: Hachette, 1877.
Gilson, Etienne. "Rabelais franciscain," in *Les Idées et les lettres.* Paris: Vrin, 1932, pp. 197-241.
Glauser, Alfred. *Rabelais créateur.* Paris: Nizet, 1966.
Gombrich, E. H. "Botticelli's Mythologies: A Study in the Neoplatonic Symbolism of his Circle," *Journal of the Warburg and Courtauld Institutes,* 8 (1945), 7-60.
———. "Icones Symbolicae: The Visual Image in Neo-Platonic Thought," *Journal of the Warburg and Courtauld Institutes,* 11 (1948), 163-192.
Gray, Floyd. "Ambiguity and Point of view in the Prologue to *Gargantua,*" *Romanic Review,* 56 (1965), 12-21.
———. "Structure and Meaning in the Prologue to the *Tiers Livre,*" *L'Esprit Créateur,* 3 (1963), 57-62.
Green, Thomas M. *Rabelais: A Study in Comic Courage.* Englewood Cliffs, N. J.: Prentiss-Hall, 1970.
Grube, G. M. A. *Plato's Thought.* London: Methuen, 1935.
Gruber, Vivian M. "Rabelais: The Didactics of Moderation," *L'Esprit Créateur,* 3 (1963), 80-86.
Guiton, Jean. "Le Mythe des paroles gelées," *Romanic Review,* 31 (1940), 3-15.
Huguet, Edmond. *Etude sur la syntaxe de Rabelais...* Paris: Hachette, 1894.
Huizinga, Johann. *Erasmus and the Age of Reformation.* Translated by F. Hopman. New York and Evanston: Harper and Row, 1957.
———. *Homo Ludens: A Study of the Play-Element in Culture.* Boston: Beacon, 1962.
Jourda, Pierre. *Le Gargantua de Rabelais.* Paris: Sfelt, 1948.
Kahn, Charles H. "A New Look at Heraclitus," *American Philosophical Quarterly,* I (1964), 189-209.
Kaiser, Walter. *Praisers of Folly: Erasmus, Rabelais, Shakespeare.* Cambridge: Harvard University Press, 1963.
Katz, Joseph. *The Philosophy of Plotinus.* New York: Appleton-Century-Crofts, 1950.
Kaufman, Walter. *Nietzsche: Philosopher, Psychologist, Antichrist.* Cleveland: Meridian Books, 1961.
Keller, Abraham C. "Pace and Timing in Rabelais' Stories," *Studies in the Renaissance,* 10 (1963), 108-125.
———. "The Books and Stories of Rabelais," *Romanic Review,* 53 (1962), 241-259.
———. "The Geophysics of Rabelais' Frozen Words," *Renaissance and Other Studies in Honor of W. L. Wilie.* Edited by George Daniel. Chapel Hill: University of North Carolina Press, 1968, pp. 151-165.
———. *The Telling of Tales in Rabelais.* Frankfurt: Vittorio Klostermann, 1963.
Kelley, Donald R. *Foundations of Modern Historical Scholarship: Language Law and History in the French Renaissance.* New York & London: Columbia University Press, 1970.
Klibansky, Raymond. *The Continuity of the Platonic Tradition during the Middle Ages.* London: The Warburg Institute, 1939.
Krailsheimer, Alban J. " 'Les Andouilles' of the *Quart Livre,*" *François Rabelais: Ouvrage publié pour le quatrième centenaire de sa mort: 1553-1953.* Geneva-Lille: Droz, 1953, pp. 227-232.

Krailsheimer, Alban J. *Rabelais*. Paris: Desclée de Brouwer, 1967.
——. *Rabelais and the Franciscans*. Oxford: Clarendon Press, 1963.
——. "Rabelais and the Pan Legend," *French Studies*, 2 (1948), 158-161.
——. "The Significance of the Pan Legend in Rabelais' Thought," *Modern Language Review*, 56 (1961), 13-23.
Kristeller, Paul Oskar. *Renaissance Thought: The Classic, Scholastic and Humanist Strains*. New York: Harper and Row, 1961.
——. *Renaissance Thought II: Papers on Humanism and the Arts*. New York: Harper and Row, 1965.
——. *Studies in Renaissance Thought and Letters*. Roma: Storia e Letteratura, 1956.
——. *The Philosophy of Marsilio Ficino*. Translated by Virginia Conant. New York: Columbia University Press, 1943.
Larmat, Jean. *Le Moyen Age dans le Gargantua de Rabelais*. Paris: Les Belles Lettres, 1973.
Lebègue, Raymond. "L'Ecolier limousin," *Revue des Cours et Conférences*, 40 (1939-1940), 303-314.
——. "Le Personnage de Pantagruel dans les *Tiers et Quart Livres*," *François Rabelais: Ouvrage publié pour le quatrième centenaire de sa mort: 1553-1953*. Geneva-Lille: Droz, 1953, pp. 164-170.
Lefebvre, Henri. *Rabelais*. Paris: Editeurs français réunis, 1955.
Lefranc, Abel. *Grands écrivains français de la renaissance*. Paris: Champion, 1914.
——. "Le Platon de Rabelais," *Bulletin du Bibliophile et du Bibliothécaire* (1901), 105-114, 169-181.
——. *Rabelais: études sur Gargantua, Pantagruel, le Tiers Livre*. Avant-propos de Robert Marichal. Paris: Michel, 1953.
——. "Un prétendu Ve Livre de Rabelais," *Revue des Etudes Rabelaisiennes*, I (1903), 29-54, 122-142.
Lévi-Strauss, Claude. *Anthropologie structurale*. Paris: Plon, 1958.
——. *La Pensée sauvage*. Paris: Plon, 1962.
Lewis, D. B. Wyndham. *Doctor Rabelais*. New York: Sheed and Ward, 1957.
Lonigan, Paul. "Rabelais' *Pantagruélion*," *Studi Francesi*, 12 (1968), 73-79.
Lote, Georges. *La Vie et l'oeuvre de François Rabelais*. Paris: Droz, 1938.
Marichal, Robert. "L'Attitude de Rabelais devant le Néoplatonisme et l'italianisme (*Quart Livre*, Ch. ix-xi)," *François Rabelais: Ouvrage publié pour le quatrième centenaire de sa mort: 1553-1953*. Geneva-Lille: Droz, 1953, pp. 181-209.
——. "*Quart Livre* — Commentaires (Note sur Gaster)," *Etudes Rabelaisiennes*, I (1956), 183-202.
Masters, G. Mallary. "The Hermetic and Platonic Tradition and Rabelais' *Dive Bouteille*," *Studi Francesi*, 10 (1966), 15-29.
——. *Rabelaisian Dialectic and the Platonic-Hermetic Tradition*. Albany: State University of New York Press, 1969.
——. "Rabelais and Renaissance Figure Poems," *Etudes Rabelaisiennes*, 8 (1969), 53-68.
Mayer, C. A. "Rabelais' Satirical Eulogy: The Praise of Borrowing and Lending," in *François Rabelais: Ouvrage publié pour le quatrième centenaire de sa mort: 1553-1953*. Geneva-Lille: Droz, 1953, pp. 147-155.
Mayer, C. A. and Douglas, C. M. "Rabelais poète," *Bibliothèque d'Humanisme et Renaissance*, 24 (1962), 42-46.

Merrill, Robert V. and Clements, Robert J. *Platonism in French Renaissance Poetry*. New York: New York University Press, 1957.
Mettra, Claude. *Rabelais secret*. Paris: Grasset, 1973.
Mossé-Bastide, Rose-Marie. *Bergson et Plotin*. Paris: Presses Universitaires de France, 1959.
Nelson, John Charles. *Renaissance Theories of Love*. New York: Columbia University Press, 1958.
Nykrog, Per. "Thélème, Panurge et la Dive Bouteille," *Revue d'Histoire Littéraire de la France*, 65 (1965), 385-397.
Panofsky, Irwin. *Idea*. Translated by Joseph Peake. Columbia: University of South Carolina Press, 1968.
Paris, Jean. *Hamlet et Panurge*. Paris: Seuil, 1971.
———. *Rabelais au futur*. Paris: Editions du Seuil, 1970.
Pelikan, Jaroslav. *The Light of the World*. New York: Harper, 1962.
Phillips, Margaret Mann. *The Adages of Erasmus: A Study with Translations*. Cambridge: Eng.: The University Press, 1964.
Pistorius, Phillippus V. *Plotinus and Neoplatonism: An Introductory Study*. Cambridge, Eng.: Bowes & Bowes, 1952.
Plattard, Jean: *François Rabelais*. Paris: Boivin, 1932.
———. *L'Invention et la composition dans l'oeuvre de Rabelais*. Paris: Champion, 1909.
———. *L'Oeuvre de Rabelais*. Paris: Champion, 1910.
———. "Rabelais et Mellin de St. Gelais," *Revue des Etudes Rabelaisiennes*, 9 (1911), 90-108.
———. "Rabelais réputé poète," *Revue des Etudes Rabelaisiennes*, 10 (1912), 291-304.
Pons, Emile. "Les 'Jargons' de Panurge dans Rabelais," *Revue de Littérature Comparée*, 11 (1931), 185-218.
Porter, Lambert C. *La Fatrasie et le fatras: Essai sur la poésie irrationnelle en France au Moyen Age*. Geneva: Droz; Paris: Minard, 1960.
Powys, John Cowper. *Rabelais*. London: Bodley Head, 1948.
Praz, Mario: *Studies in Seventeenth-Century Imagery*. Rome: Edizioni di Storia e Letteratura, 1964, 2nd ed.
Putnam, Samuel. *François Rabelais, Man of the Renaissance, A Spiritual Biography*. New York: Cape and Smith, 1929.
Renaudet, Augustin. *Préréforme et humanisme à Paris pendant les premières guerres d'Italie (1494-1517)*. Paris: Champion, 1916.
Rigolot, François. *Les Langages de Rabelais*. Geneva: Droz, 1972.
Sainéan, Lazare. *L'Influence et la réputation de Rabelais*. Paris: Gamber, 1930.
———. *La Langue de Rabelais*. Paris: Boccard, 1922-1923. 2 vols.
Saulnier, Verdun L. *Le Dessein de Rabelais*. Paris: Société d'édition d'enseignement supérieur, 1957.
———. "L'Enigme du Pantagruélion," *Etudes Rabelaisiennes*, I (1956), 48-72.
———. "Hommes pétrifiés et pierres vives (Autour d'une formule de Panurge)," *Bibliothèque d'Humanisme et Renaissance*, 24 (1960), 393-402.
———. "Pantagruel au large de Ganabin et la peur de Panurge," *Bibliothèque d'Humanisme et Renaissance*, 16 (1954), 58-81.
———. "Rabelais devant l'écolier limousin," *Mercure de France* (October, 1948), 269-275.

Saulnier, Verdun L. "Le Silence de Rabelais et le mythe des paroles gelées," *François Rabelais: Ouvrage publié pour le quatrième centenaire de sa mort: 1553-1953*. Geneva-Lille: Droz, 1953, pp. 233-247.
Screech, M. A. "Emblems and Colours: The Controversy over Gargantua's Colours and Devices," *Mélanges d'histoire offerts à Henri Meylan*. Geneva: Droz, 1970.
———. *L'Evangélisme de Rabelais: Aspects de la satire religieuse au XVI⁰ siècle*. Geneva-Lille: Droz, 1959.
———. "The Meaning of Thaumaste," *Bibliothèque d'Humanisme et Renaissance*, 22 (1960), 62-72.
———. *The Rabelaisian Marriage: Aspects of Rabelais's Religion, Ethics and Comic Philosophy*. London: Arnold, 1958.
———. "The Sense of Rabelais's Enigme en prophétie," *Bibliothèque d'Humanisme et Renaissance*, 18 (1956), 393-404.
Selig, Karl Ludwig. "Emblem Literature: Directions in Recent Scholarship," *Yearbook of Comparative and General Literature*, 12 (1963), 36-41.
Smith, W. F. "Rabelais on Language by Sign," *Modern Language Review*, 8 (1913), 193-198.
Snyder, Solomon H. "What We Have Forgotten about Pot — A Pharmacologist's History." *The New York Times Magazine*, Dec. 13. 1970.
Spanos, Margaret. "The Function of the Prologues in the Works of Rabelais," *Etudes Rabelaisiennes*, 9 (1971), 29-48.
Spitzer, Leo. *Classical and Christian Ideas of World Harmony: Prolegomena to an Interpretation of the Word "Stimmung,"* Edited by Anna Granville Hatcher. Baltimore: Johns Hopkins, 1963.
———. "Ancora sul prologo al primo libro del *Gargantua* di Rabelais," *Studi Francesi*, 9 (1965), 423-434.
———. *Linguistics and Literary History*. Princeton: Princeton University Press, 1963.
———. "Le Prétendu Réalisme de Rabelais," *Modern Philology*, 37 (1939-1940), 139-150.
———. "Rabelais et les 'rabelaisants'," *Studi Francesi*, 4 (1960), 401-423.
———. "The Works of Rabelais," in *Literary Masterpieces of the Western World*. Edited by Francis H. Horn. Baltimore: Johns Hopkins, 1953, pp. 126-147.
Stapfer, Paul. *Rabelais, sa personne, son génie, son oeuvre...* Paris: Colin, 1889.
Starobinski, Jean. "Note sur Rabelais et le langage," *Tel quel*, 15 (1963), 79-81.
Taylor, A. E. *Plato, the Man and his Work*. London: Methuen, 1948.
Telle, Emile V. "L'Isle des Alliances (Quart Livre, Chap. ix) ou l'Anti-Thélème," *Bibliothèque d'Humanisme et Renaissance*, 14 (1952), 159-175.
———. "Thélème et le Paulinisme matrimonial Erasmien: Le sens de l'Enigme en prophétie," in *François Rabelais: Ouvrage publié pour le quatrième centenaire de sa mort*: Geneva-Lille: Droz, 1953, pp. 104-119.
Tetel, Marcel. "Aspects du comique dans les images de Rabelais," *L'Esprit Créateur*, 3 (1963), 51-56.
———. *Etude sur le comique de Rabelais*. Florence: Olschki, 1964.
———. "La fin du Quart Livre," *Romanische Forschungen*, 83 (1971), 517-527.
———. *Rabelais*. New York: Twayne, 1967.
———. "La Valeur comique des accumulations verbales chez Rabelais," *Romanic Review*, 53 (1962), 96-104.

Thomas, Jean. "Diderot et Rabelais," *Revue du Seizième Siècle*, 19 (1933), 323-324.
Thorndike, Lynn. *A History of Magic and Experimental Science*. New York: Columbia University Press, 1923-1941. 8 vols.
Thuasne, Louis. *Etudes sur Rabelais*. Paris: Bouillon, 1904.
Tilley, Arthur. *François Rabelais*. Philadelphia-London: Lippincott, 1907.
Vallet, Nicolas, "Rabelais, le livre et le vin," *Revue des langues romances*, 78 (1969), 197-212.
Villey-Desmeserets, Pierre. *Marot et Rabelais*. Vol. I of *Les Grands écrivains du XVIe siècle*. Paris: Champion, 1923.
Walker, Daniel P. "Orpheus the Theologian and Renaissance Platonists," *Journal of the Warburg and Courtauld Institutes*, 16 (1953), 100-120.
Weinberg, Bernard. "Rabelais as an Artist," *Texas Quarterly*, 3 (1960), 175-188.
Weinberg, Florence. *The Wine and the Will*. Detroit: Wayne State Univ. Press, 1972.
Willcocks, Mary. *The Laughing Philosopher, Being a Life of François Rabelais*. London: Allen and Unwin, 1950.
Wind, Edgar. *Pagan Mysteries in the Renaissance*. Harmondsworth, England: Penguin Books, 1967.
Wolfson, Harry A. "Extradeical and Intradeical Interpretations of Platonic Ideas," *Journal of the History of Ideas*, 22 (1961), 23-32.
Zabeeh, Farhang. *Universals: A New Look at an Old Problem*. The Hague: Martinus Nijhoff, 1966.
Zeldin, Jesse. "The Abbey and the Bottle," *L'Esprit Créateur*, 3 (1963), 68-74.

NORTH CAROLINA STUDIES IN THE ROMANCE LANGUAGES AND LITERATURES

I.S.B.N. Prefix 0-8078-

Recent Titles

FRANCIS PETRARCH, SIX CENTURIES LATER, by Aldo Scaglione. 1975. (No. 159).
STYLE AND STRUCTURE IN GRACIÁN'S "EL CRITICÓN"; by Marcia L. Welles. 1976. (No. 160). *-007-6*.
MOLIERE: TRADITIONS IN CRITICISM, by Laurence Romero. 1974 (Essays, No. 1). *-001-7*.
CHRÉTIEN'S JEWISH GRAIL. A NEW INVESTIGATION OF THE IMAGERY AND SIGNIFICANCE OF CHRÉTIEN DE TROYES'S GRAIL EPISODE BASED UPON MEDIEVAL HEBRAIC SOURCES, by Eugene J. Weinraub. 1976. (Essays, No. 2). *-002-5*.
STUDIES IN TIRSO, I, by Ruth Lee Kennedy. 1974. (Essays, No. 3). *-003-3*.
VOLTAIRE AND THE FRENCH ACADEMY, by Karlis Racevskis. 1975. (Essays, No. 4). *-004-1*.
THE NOVELS OF MME RICCOBONI, by Joan Hinde Stewart. 1976. (Essays, No. 8). *-008-4*.
FIRE AND ICE: THE POETRY OF XAVIER VILLAURRUTIA, by Merlin H. Forster. 1976. (Essays, No. 11). *-011-4*.
THE THEATER OF ARTHUR ADAMOV, by John J. McCann. 1975. (Essays, No. 13). *-013-0*.
AN ANATOMY OF POESIS: THE PROSE POEMS OF STÉPHANE MALLARMÉ, by Ursula Franklin. 1976. (Essays, No. 16). *-016-5*.
LAS MEMORIAS DE GONZALO FERNÁNDEZ DE OVIEDO, Vols. I and II, by Juan Bautista Avalle-Arce. 1974. (Texts, Textual Studies, and Translations, Nos. 1 and 2). *-401-2; 402-0*.
GIACOMO LEOPARDI: THE WAR OF THE MICE AND THE CRABS, translated, introduced and annotated by Ernesto G. Caserta. 1976. (Texts, Textual Studies, and Translations, No. 4). *-404-7*.
LUIS VÉLEZ DE GUEVARA: A CRITICAL BIBLIOGRAPHY, by Mary G. Hauer. 1975. (Texts, Textual Studies, and Translations, No. 5). *-405-5*.
UN TRÍPTICO DEL PERÚ VIRREINAL: "EL VIRREY AMAT, EL MARQUÉS DE SOTO FLORIDO Y LA PERRICHOLI". EL "DRAMA DE DOS PALANGANAS" Y SU CIRCUNSTANCIA, estudio preliminar, reedición y notas por Guillermo Lohmann Villena. 1976. (Texts, Textual Studies, and Translation, No. 15). *-415-2*.
LOS NARRADORES HISPANOAMERICANOS DE HOY, edited by Juan Bautista Avalle-Arce. 1973. (Symposia, No. 1). *-951-0*.
ESTUDIOS DE LITERATURA HISPANOAMERICANA EN HONOR A JOSÉ J. ARROM, edited by Andrew P. Debicki and Enrique Pupo-Walker. 1975. (Symposia, No. 2). *-952-9*.
MEDIEVAL MANUSCRIPTS AND TEXTUAL CRITICISM, edited by Christopher Kleinhenz. 1976. (Symposia, No. 4). *-954-5*.
SAMUEL BECKETT. THE ART OF RHETORIC. edited by Edouard Morot-Sir. Howard Harper, and Dougald McMillan III. 1976. (Symposia, No. 5). *-955-3*.
DELIE. CONCORDANCE, by Jerry Nash. 1976. 2 Volumes. (No. 174).
FIGURES OF REPETITION IN THE OLD PROVENÇAL LYRIC: A STUDY IN THE STYLE OF THE TROUBADOURS, by Nathaniel B. Smith. 1976. (No. 176). *-9176-2*.
A CRITICAL EDITION OF LE REGIME TRESUTILE ET TRESPROUFITABLE POUR CONSERVER ET GARDER LA SANTE DU CORPS HUMAIN, by Patricia Willett Cummins. 1977. (No. 177).
THE DRAMA OF SELF IN GUILLAUME APOLLINAIRE'S "ALCOOLS", by Richard Howard Stamelman. 1976. (No. 178). *-9178-9*.
A CRITICAL EDITION OF "LA PASSION NOSTRE SEIGNEUR" FROM MANUSCRIPT 1131 FROM THE BIBLIOTHEQUE SAINTE-GENEVIEVE, PARIS, by Edward J. Gallagher. 1976. (No. 179). *-9179-7*.

When ordering please cite the *ISBN Prefix* plus the last four digits for each title.

Send orders to: University of North Carolina Press
North Carolina 27514
Chapel Hill
U S. A

NORTH CAROLINA STUDIES IN THE ROMANCE LANGUAGES AND LITERATURES

I.S.B.N. Prefix 0-8078-

Recent Titles

A QUANTITATIVE AND COMPARATIVE STUDY OF THE VOCALISM OF THE LATIN INSCRIPTIONS OF NORTH AFRICA, BRITAIN, DALMATIA, AND THE BALKANS, by Stephen William Omeltchenko. 1977. (No. 180). -9180-0.

OCTAVIEN DE SAINT-GELAIS "LE SEJOUR D'HONNEUR", edited by Joseph A. James. 1977. (No. 181). -9181-9.

A STUDY OF NOMINAL INFLECTION IN LATIN INSCRIPTIONS, by Paul A. Gaeng. 1977. (No. 182). -9182-7.

THE LIFE AND WORKS OF LUIS CARLOS LÓPEZ, by Martha S. Bazik. 1977. (No. 183). -9183-5.

"THE CORT D'AMOR". A THIRTEENTH-CENTURY ALLEGORICAL ART OF LOVE, by Lowanne E. Jones. 1977. (No. 185). -9185-1.

PHYTONYMIC DERIVATIONAL SYSTEMS IN THE ROMANCE LANGUAGES: STUDIES IN THEIR ORIGIN AND DEVELOPMENT, by Walter E. Geiger. 1978. (No. 187). -9187-8.

LANGUAGE IN GIOVANNI VERGA'S EARLY NOVELS, by Nicholas Patruno. 1977. (No. 188). -9188-6.

BLAS DE OTERO EN SU POESÍA, by Moraima de Semprún Donahue. 1977. (No. 189). -9189-4.

LA ANATOMÍA DE "EL DIABLO COJUELO": DESLINDES DEL GÉNERO ANATOMÍSTICO, por C. George Peale. 1977. (No. 191). -9191-6.

RICHARD SANS PEUR, EDITED FROM "LE ROMANT DE RICHART" AND FROM GILLES CORROZET'S "RICHART SANS PAOUR", by Denis Joseph Conlon. 1977. (No. 192). -9192-4.

MARCEL PROUST'S GRASSET PROOFS. *Commentary and Variants*, by Douglas Alden. 1978. (No. 193). -9193-2.

MONTAIGNE AND FEMINISM, by Cecile Insdorf. 1977. (No. 194). -9194-0.

SANTIAGO F. PUGLIA, AN EARLY PHILADELPHIA PROPAGANDIST FOR SPANISH AMERICAN INDEPENDENCE, by Merle S. Simmons. 1977. (No. 195). -9195-9.

BAROQUE FICTION-MAKING. A STUDY OF GOMBERVILLE'S "POLEXANDRE", by Edward Baron Turk. 1978. (No. 196). -9196-7.

THE TRAGIC FALL: DON ÁLVARO DE LUNA AND OTHER FAVORITES IN SPANISH GOLDEN AGE DRAMA, by Raymond R. MacCurdy. 1978. (No. 197). -9197-5.

A BAHIAN HERITAGE. An Ethnolinguistic Study of African Influences on Bahian Portuguese, by William W. Megenney. 1978. (No. 198). -9198-3.

"LA QUERELLE DE LA ROSE: Letters and Documents", by Joseph L. Baird and John R. Kane. 1978. (No. 199). -9199-1.

TWO AGAINST TIME. *A Study of the very present worlds of Paul Claudel and Charles Péguy*, by Joy Nachod Humes. 1978. (No. 200). -9200-9.

TECHNIQUES OF IRONY IN ANATOLE FRANCE. Essay on *Les sept femmes de la Barbe-Bleue*, by Diane Wolfe Levy. 1978. (No. 201). -9201-7.

THE PERIPHRASTIC FUTURES FORMED BY THE ROMANCE REFLEXES OF "VADO (AD)" "PLUS INFINITIVE, by James Joseph Champion. 1978 (No. 202). -9202-5.

THE EVOLUTION OF THE LATIN /b/-/u̯/ MERGER: A Quantitative and Comparative Analysis of the B-V Alternation in Latin Inscriptions, by Joseph Louis Barbarino. 1978 (No. 203). -9203-3.

METAPHORIC NARRATION: THE STRUCTURE AND FUNCTION OF METAPHORS IN "A LA RECHERCHE DU TEMPS PERDU", by Inge Karalus Crosman. 1978 (No. 204). -9204-1.

RABELAIS: HOMO LOGOS, by Alice Fiola Berry. 1979. (No. 208). -9208-4.

When ordering please cite the *ISBN Prefix* plus the last four digits for each title.

Send orders to: University of North Carolina Press
                  Chapel Hill
                  North Carolina 27514
                  U. S. A.

The Department of Romance Studies Digital Arts and Collaboration Lab at the University of North Carolina at Chapel Hill is proud to support the digitization of the North Carolina Studies in the Romance Languages and Literatures series.

www.ingramcontent.com/pod-product-compliance
Lightning Source LLC
Chambersburg PA
CBHW030237240426
43663CB00037B/1239